£2.00

£2.00

VEGETABLE GARDENING

Hamlyn Practical Gardening Guides

VEGETABLE GARDENING

David Toyne

HAMLYN

Published in 1989 by
The Hamlyn Publishing Group Limited
a division of the Octopus Publishing Group
Michelin House
81 Fulham Road
London SW3 6RB

© 1989 The Hamlyn Publishing Group Limited

ISBN 0 600 564 800

Typeset by MS Filmsetting Limited, Frome, Somerset
Printed in Italy

CONTENTS

With clever planning and the use of modern cultivation methods, it is possible to grow an impressive selection of vegetables in a modest-sized garden.

INTRODUCTION

While it is true to say that your local greengrocer or supermarket can provide all the vegetables you need and, often, tropical varieties flown in as well, there are good reasons for growing your own.

First, there is something very special about the taste of a vegetable picked just before it goes into the pot – however good transport and storage facilities are, shop-bought produce just cannot match it. Second, you can grow varieties that are not available from the retail trade, with better and different flavours. Third, the fresh air and exercise obtained while working on the plot is highly therapeutic. And finally, you will also be saving money.

It was reckoned that the traditional allotment plot of 27·5 m × 9 m (90 ft × 30 ft) would provide a family of four with vegetables for a whole year. The development of heavier cropping varieties and new techniques in cultivation, however, now make it possible to grow a sufficient quantity of vegetables in the much smaller area you are likely to be able to set aside in today's more modest gardens.

CHOOSING THE SITE

The ideal place for a vegetable garden is an open but not exposed site, sheltered by walls to the north and east. It also has a slight slope towards the south without a restricting wall on that side to trap cold air in winter, so forming a frost pocket. We would all like the opportunity of picking such a site, but usually we are faced with the garden we have. It is therefore comforting to know that, provided the site is not too over-shadowed or exposed, good crops of most vegetables can be grown without too much difficulty.

As few vegetables will tolerate shade to any degree, a good deal of sunlight is preferable, so your plot should be kept away from the shade cast by houses or large trees. Also, remember that the spreading roots of trees steal water and food from your crops.

Vegetables grown in rows have a formality which may not fit in with the rest of the garden and it is generally accepted that they are best grown in a separate plot, hidden behind a screen or hedge, along with a compost heap and a cold frame. However, there has been a recent revival of the geometrically designed vegetable plot with square, rectangular or diamond-shaped beds intersected by brick or paving-slab paths, much like the traditional herb garden. These feature gardens may even take the place of the main ornamental garden.

Combining vegetables with ornamental plants is also becoming popular in small gardens. Walls or fences can support runner beans and peas, and small beds – perhaps with courgettes or sweet corn – can be integrated with the flower garden. The more unruly vegetables, like cabbages and broad beans are, however, still kept discreetly tucked away in the traditional plot.

Undoubtedly, if you are able to start from scratch either with a virgin garden or by moving an existing vegetable plot, it is easier to meet more of the ideal requirements and to ensure that the rows of vegetables run north to south to avoid one row shading another.

DECIDING WHAT TO GROW

Whether your aim is to supply your family with vegetables for the whole year or just to grow a few special varieties, several factors must be taken into account.

CLIMATE
Local climatic conditions can vary within a relatively short distance, and although varieties have been specially bred for the colder conditions of the north, certain crops may still not be successful in those areas, in higher places, or even in normally favourable areas if the garden has the wrong aspect and is exposed to a prevailing wind. To help you make the right choice the A–Z of Vegetables (see pages 37 to 75) gives details of suitable varieties and their hardiness.

Despite these restrictions, vegetable gardening is full of surprises and it may be worth trying a crop that is theoretically unsuitable, especially if you can first raise strong plants in a greenhouse and provide protection in the garden with cloches.

SPACE
The amount of space you have is an important factor in deciding what to grow. With an area 18 m × 6 m (60 ft × 20 ft) it is certainly possible for today's average family to have fresh vegetables all the year. By using intensive cropping methods (see Managing the Plot) the area required for self-sufficiency can be considerably reduced.

With only a small space available, however, it would be better to grow the rarer, more expensive crops, like asparagus, or varieties of ordinary vegetables with lower yields but superb flavour, such as the potato 'Epicure'.

If you are lucky enough to have space for a full-sized plot, long-term storage, thanks to the introduction of the domestic deep-freeze, is no longer a problem.

Potatoes and onions can be stored for several months in a frost-free shed. If you bury carrots or beetroot in boxes of peat or sand they will also keep for some time.

TIME
Another limiting factor, although less tangible than the others, is the time you can spare for the necessary operations. Beginners will take much longer than experienced gardeners to carry out the same tasks, and some crops need more attention than others – celery, for example. Because the plot size and intensiveness of cropping are variable, it is difficult to be specific, but an hour a day, or its equivalent each week, will certainly produce satisfactory results in all but the largest vegetable plot.

PREPARING THE PLOT

The area chosen for the vegetable garden is often grassed over – either as old pasture in the case of a new estate, or as a lawn in an established garden. The former will contain perennial weeds, and both will have pests that must be dealt with.

An established lawn that has been regularly mown is the basis of that legendary material called loam and, provided it is relatively free of deep-rooted perennial weeds, you can use it for making your own seed or potting compost. This is done by skimming about 2·5 cm (1 in) of the turf off your proposed plot with a spade and stacking it upside down in neat layers in a sheltered corner of the garden. After decaying for two or three years, it will have become rich fibrous loam.

DIGGING THE PLOT

If you do not wish to make use of the turf in this way, mark out the plot and skim off one spade's width and set it aside. Next, remove the soil to make a trench the depth of a spade blade and also set this aside. Then skim off the turf from the next spade width and turn it in the previous trench before covering it with the soil from the second trench. Proceed in this

Garden spades and forks come in a variety of sizes so use ones suited to both your strength and your height. When not in use, try to keep them clean and wipe the metal parts with an oily rag once a year.

SINGLE DIGGING

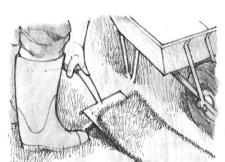

1. After marking out the plot, skim off a strip of turf, one spade wide. Set the turf aside to place in the final trench.

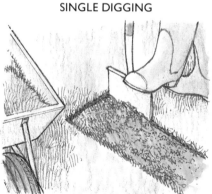

2. Dig out the soil to one spade's depth and place it in a wheelbarrow – it will be used at the end of the job in the final trench.

3. Make a second trench, turning the turf and soil from it into the initial trench. Repeat, and fill final trench with topsoil from wheelbarrow.

HOW TO DIG CORRECTLY

1. First, chop at right angles to the trench, marking out only a small bite at a time.

2. Holding the spade vertically, and placing one foot on the tread, cut down parallel to the trench.

3. Slipping one hand down to the base of the handle, turn the clod over into the previous trench.

Double digging is only necessary once every ten years or so on compacted soils. After making a trench to one blade's depth, loosen the soil at the bottom with a fork.

manner until you have dug the last trench, and fill it with the turf and soil you originally put aside. This is called single digging.

On very compacted soils double digging is necessary, perhaps just once in several years. This involves loosening the soil at the bottom of the trench to a further spade's depth, before turning in soil from the next trench.

If you are making your plot from pasture or an old lawn that is full of perennial weeds it is best to spray the area first with a safe, total weedkiller. Such a weedkiller is taken up by the foliage and transported through the plant, but is inactivated by the soil and therefore leaves no harmful residues.

CHOOSING IMPLEMENTS AND DIGGING TECHNIQUES

A good, sharp spade is the usual implement, although a fork may be better for clay or stony soil and is essential for loosening the bottom of trenches and for double digging. Spades and forks vary in length and weight so you should choose one tool with the combination that suits you and the job best.

Digging is probably the most strenuous work there is in the garden. If you are out of practice, take it easy for the first couple of days until your back and muscles get used to it. Take a small 'bite' at a time with the spade or fork, chopping at right angles to the trench before cutting down parallel to it with the spade's blade or fork's tines held vertically. Then turn the squarish clod forwards and over into the previously made trench. You will soon find how much soil you can comfortably handle, and which of the implements is more suitable for your soil. As the days go by you will find that you can do more and more digging at a time.

WHEN TO DIG

Autumn or early winter are usually regarded as the best times for this operation so that ensuing frosts can break down the rough clods. This is really only true on heavy soils; the lighter ones are often best dug in spring. Heavy winter rains 'puddle' the surface and when this dries out a hard 'cap' may be formed. This prevents weed seedling emergence, and vigorous raking will soon break it up to form a seed bed ready for sowing.

By incorporating manure into the soil, you improve its fertility and its structure. Dig it in, either in autumn or winter.

FEEDING THE SOIL

Growing plants take a lot of goodness from the soil which must be replaced, especially in the vegetable garden where most of the produce is harvested and therefore unavailable for composting.

MANURE, COMPOST AND FERTILIZERS

The value to the soil of manure or compost is two-fold. First, it physically improves all types of soils – from light, free-draining, chalky or sandy soils to heavy, wet, sticky clay. It holds together light free-draining soils, giving them more substance, and opens up heavy soils to provide better drainage. It also introduces air spaces and absorbent reservoirs which hold water and nutrients in readiness for the plants.

Second, manure or compost provides a fertile breeding ground for micro-organisms, such as beneficial bacteria and fungi, and larger creatures like worms. All of these play their part in digesting the organic material to release its nutrients, and forming humus which improves the soil's texture and workability. However, for the best yields of top quality produce, you must add more nutrients than are provided by manure or compost alone. A combination of compost or manure and fertilizer is ideal.

The nutrients vital for all plants are divided into three groups: major, inter-mediate, and trace elements.

MAJOR NUTRIENTS

There are three major nutrients:
Nitrogen Often called 'the leaf maker', this is vital for all green parts of the plant.
Phosphate Known as 'the root maker', this nutrient is also essential for converting the energy of sunlight into plant growth.
Potash This – 'the flower and fruit maker' – is principally needed for its role in carbohydrate (starch and sugar) production which gives fruit and vegetables their flavour, promotes ripeness, hardiness, and drought and disease resistance.

These three, often abbreviated to NPK, are used in quite large quantities. Note, however, that unlike nitrogen, which can be used 'straight' by plants, phosphate is given to plants as P_2O_5 (phosphorus pentoxide) and potash as K_2O (potassium oxide). It is these formulae that you will see printed on the bags of fertilizer sold to amateur gardeners.

Intermediate nutrients These – magnesium, calcium and sulphur – are used in smaller amounts. They are not normally lacking in soils, but magnesium, in particular, is essential to soils already rich in potash. It is also necessary if you are growing tomatoes, for example, which require extra large amounts.

Trace elements These include iron, manganese, boron, zinc and copper, of which only minute amounts of each are required by plants. Soils in this country do not generally suffer from deficiencies of trace elements, but if they do, it is usually manganese, which is always worth providing. Usually manure or compost can provide virtually all the trace elements needed by vegetables.

APPLYING FERTILIZERS

Fertilizers are sold as 'straights', like sulphate of ammonia, which contains only one major nutrient (in this case, nitrogen) or as 'compounds', which contain two or more major nutrients and sometimes various combinations of intermediate nutrients and trace elements. Unless you suspect that one of the major nutrients is missing from your soil, it is easier to use

APPLYING FERTILIZER

Base dressing: before sowing or planting rake a dry base dressing into the soil. For application rates, follow the manufacturer's instructions carefully.

Dry top dressing: this is sprinkled around the plants once they are growing. If it does not rain for a few days after applying, water it in.

Liquid top dressing: dilute liquid fertilizers before use, according to quantities given by the manufacturer. Apply around the base of the plant, using a watering can.

the compound types, which are readily available and cheap. This particularly applies to the soluble fertilizers which, being concentrated, are even greater value for money.

Whether the source of a fertilizer is inorganic (naturally occurring or manufactured minerals) or organic (derived from animal or plant materials) its constituents, when in the soil, become solutions of inorganic salts, which is the only form that can be absorbed by the plant.

There are two ways of applying fertilizers: as a base dressing or as a top dressing. A base dressing is applied to the soil before planting or sowing, and is usually either raked or forked in. Top dressings are subsequent applications of fertilizers, either dry or liquid, given to growing plants.

To help you make a choice of fertilizer, the chart below compares the major nutrient and trace elements content, and speed of action – fast, medium, slow or very slow – of several popular and readily available fertilizers.

BASE DRESSING – WHICH AND HOW MUCH?

The type and quantity of fertilizer depends on the answers to three questions:
● Have you dug your plot from previously grass-covered land?
● What type of soil do you have?
● What crops do you wish to grow?

Previously grass covered If the answer to the first question is 'Yes', this is a special case. Because grass is an efficient remover of potash from the soil, old lawns or pasture will be more deficient in this nutrient the older they are, so when your plot is cultivated for the first time, a heavy dressing of potash is essential for raising

PLANT FOODS IN GROWMORE AND ORGANIC FERTILIZERS					
Fertilizer	Major nutrients (percentage)			Other nutrients	Acting rate
	N	P_2O_5	K_2O		
Growmore	7	7	7	none	fast
Mushroom compost	0·5	0·3	0·6	calcium, magnesium	slow
Garden compost	0·4	0·2	0·5	soil improving qualities	slow
A tomato fertilizer	4	4·5	8	magnesium	slow
A general purpose organic fertilizer	7·3	5	5·2	calcium, sulphur, trace elements	slow
Dried blood	12	2	1	trace elements	fast
Blood, fish and bone	5	8	6	trace elements	medium
Hoof and horn	12	1	0	calcium, sulphur	medium
Seaweed meal	1·5	0·5	2	magnesium, calcium, sulphur, iodine, trace elements	medium
Bone meal	4	20	0	Up to 23% calcium, and magnesium, sulphur, trace elements	very slow

good crops. The simplest remedy is to use a ready-made compound fertilizer containing all three major nutrients but one in which there is a high level of potash. Such a base dressing will not cause an imbalance and can be applied over the whole area in addition to and before any other treatments.

Soil type If your soil is light chalk or sand, a heavy dressing of well rotted garden compost or farmyard manure should be dug in when making the plot, before applying the base dressing. If, however, your plot has been cut from grassland on a light soil the base dressing could be dug in at the same time as the compost or manure.

What crops? This brings us to the important matter of lime and soil pH. All rain is slightly acid and slowly dissolves the calcium (an essential nutrient) in the soil, making it more available for plants but also washing it away. Manures and some fertilizers also make calcium more available to plants so they are able to take up more of it. But heavy cropping will reduce the quantity of calcium available making the soil more acid.

For this reason vegetable gardens have, traditionally, been given an annual dressing of garden lime, ground chalk or limestone. But the extent to which soil loses calcium is often exaggerated and comparatively few soils in this country are deficient in lime (even the brassica family, which is lime-loving, does not like extremely alkaline soil). The message, therefore, is not to lime the vegetable garden every year as a matter of course.

Soil acidity or alkalinity is measured on a pH scale of 1 to 14 – pH 1 is very acid, like sulphuric acid, and pH 14 is very alkaline, like caustic soda; the middle point, pH 7, is neutral. Discovering the pH of your soil is simple with one of the pH test kits readily available. Test several areas, because the pH can change dramatically within quite a short distance.

Most soils fall between pH 4·5 and pH 7·5, although peaty soils may be lower than this and those on chalk will be higher. The chart opposite will help you to determine if lime is needed in the soil, and how much. The pH should be raised gradually by annual dressing so the recommended

yearly amount is given as well as the total amount required.

Very acid, sandy, and peaty soils may be naturally low in trace elements and liming them might induce deficiencies of these trace elements and reduce crops.

WHEN TO LIME
The most convenient time to apply lime is in autumn, but as manure and fertilizer do not mix with lime this would depend on when these other two are used. The simple rule is to lime only the cabbage patch, which, if the standard crop rotation is used (see pages 25 to 28), will mean each area of the plot will be limed once in three years. The manure and fertilizer can then be dug in during the following spring when the lime has been weathered into the soil.

ORGANIC MANURES
In natural conditions plants die down or shed their leaves. All this material decomposes and returns valuable nutrients to the soil. In the garden we interfere with this natural process by clearing everything away – in the case of vegetables by harvesting them. In the vegetable plot, then, it is doubly important to return as much organic matter as you possibly can to the soil.

Adding organic matter, such as well rotted manure and garden compost helps to hold together light soils and breaks up heavy clay. It also encourages organisms to multiply, releasing valuable plant nutrients from the organic material and from the soil. As it decays, it leaves a residue of essential humus which continues to

Simple kits for testing the pH of your soil are readily available.

Opposite: Green manure is a quick-growing crop of alfalfa, mustard or rape which is dug into the soil just before flowering, so introducing valuable nutrients to the soil.

Scatter lime on the surface of the soil, preferably in autumn. The rain will then wash it into the ground. Never dig it in, as this would leave the soil near the surface untouched.

cold. A high nitrogen fertilizer, one of the straight nitrogen fertilizers – urea or ammonium sulphate – or rich organic matter, like cow manure, will produce much quicker results than leafmould.

During a warm autumn and from spring onwards stir or water the rotting leaves (according to type) into the heap or bin, but cover them well to keep out the rain, which could make the leaves excessively wet and reduce the speed at which they will decay.

Soil-texture improvement Leafmould is essentially a soil improver, valuable because it is slow to decay completely, rich in humus and conserves the nutrients from fertilizers. Add it to the soil at about 3 kg per sq m (5 lb per sq yd). It is almost weed-free, making it an excellent mulch for between and around vegetables.

Plant-food content One of the reasons why leaves fall from trees in the autumn is that they have returned most of their essential nutrients to the plant and can no longer sustain themselves. Thus, when made into leafmould, they have no real food value. Those from broad-leaved trees growing on alklaine soil contain a considerable amount of calcium which is beneficial to the cabbage family.

Peat This is the remains of plants which have decomposed under airless conditions in bogs and, consequently, their remains are very durable.

The durability of its contents depends on the age of the peat – some of the younger, less-decomposed ones, such as many of the Scandinavian peats available, begin to decay again quite rapidly after being added to the soil.

conserve water and the nutrients from fertilizers which may be added to the soil later on.

Not all the bulky organic materials added to the soil are equally beneficial. The term 'organic matter' includes, for example, peat and mushroom compost, both of which are widely available, but they do not have the same properties as manure or compost. Here are the benefits and shortcomings of the various types available to the gardener.

Green manure Specially sown, quick-growing crops which are dug into the soil while still growing and 'green'. Examples are mustard, rape, alfalfa, sweet clover, and Italian rye grass. Sow at about 38 g/sq m (1 oz/sq yd) and rake into the levelled soil's surface. They are grown for six to eight weeks and then dug in, usually before flowering and certainly before setting seed. Sow from March to about July, although quicker-growing mustard can be sown as late as September.

Soil-texture improvement Soft green plants decay rapidly, so green manuring must be repeated annually.

Plant-food content It provides nitrogen, especially alfalfa and sweet clover, which accumulate this element in their root nodules. These then rapidly decay to release it again. It also traps any nitrogen from a previous fertilizer dressing and prevents it being washed or leached out of

the soil. As green manure consists of immature plants, it is not a valuable source of trace elements.

Leafmould This consists of rotted-down autumn leaves. Tree and shrub leaves (especially those with large amounts of natural preservative, like plane, beech, horse chestnut and all evergreens) are slow to decay, taking more than a year to produce crumbly leafmould. Gathering them into piles or putting them in bins speeds up the process only slightly. Small quantities, however, can be successfully composted in polythene sacks – in these it is easier to ensure the leaves are thoroughly wetted before closing the top and you can store them somewhere reasonably well protected from extreme

AMOUNT OF LIME NEEDED TO RAISE SOIL pH TO 6·6						
Original pH	Clay or peat soil		Average loam soil		Light sandy soil	
	kg per sq m	lb per sq yd	kg per sq m	lb per sq yd	kg per sq m	lb per sq yd
4·0	2·7	5	1·7	4½	2	3¾
4·5	2·2	4	1·9	3½	1·6	3
5·0	1·8	3¾	1·5	2¾	1·2	2¼
5·5	1·2	2¼	1·1	2	0·8	1½
6·0	0·8	¾	0·5	1	0·4	
Annual rate	0·27	½	0·54	1	0·81	1½

Soil-texture improvement All peats are excellent and relatively long-lasting soil improvers, but only a little humus is left by the time they are completely decayed. Also, because they are light, quite large quantities are required to achieve real improvement – up to 5 kg per sq m (10 lb per sq yd) may be necessary before any benefit is felt. Peat is weed-free and sterile, making it a good mulch.

Plant-food content Major and minor plant foods are almost totally lacking in peat and most peats are quite acid, so additional lime will be necessary when they are used on acid soils with crops requiring a higher pH value.

Bark A by-product of forestry and timber production, this is sold in composted and pulverized or chipped forms. Only the finer grades of composted bark should be used in the soil. The chipped forms are only advisable as a mulch where crops are to be grown.

Soil-texture improvement Composted bark is even slower to decay than peat and, as it is an equally excellent soil improver, it is theoretically the better of the two. It is more expensive – although less is needed and a little more humus is eventually formed. Both composted and chipped barks are weed-free and good for mulching, but bear in mind chipped raw bark contains resins which inhibit seed germination so it is best used only around established plants. A 2·5 cm (1 in) layer of composted bark is recommended for digging in and a 5 cm (2 in) layer for mulching.

Plant-food content Bark provides a small quantity of trace elements, when thoroughly composted.

Farmyard manure Often abbreviated to FYM, the original cow, pig or horse manure was a mixture of dung and straw bedding. It had to be stacked and thoroughly composted before use, otherwise the tough straw content would decay in the soil using up any nitrogen present, as well as any added from fertilizers. FYM is still one of the most valuable forms of organic matter, but today wood shavings and other equally decay-resistant bedding materials are also used for animals. This means the rule to use only 'well rotted' manure is even more important.

Opposite: Always enclose the compost heap so you can make a high pile, and keep it looking neat and tidy.

Left: As peat is virtually free of weed seeds, it makes an excellent mulch. It is one of the more expensive choices, however.

Left: Composted bark makes an effective and attractive mulch for mature plants.

Marrows must be grown in soil which is rich in organic matter.

Soil-texture improvement FYM is not a long lived soil improver – about 80 per cent is used up within the first year or so, but during that time it is an excellent and rapid soil conditioner and source of humus.

Plant-food content Many factors affect its food value but, on average, two bucketfuls of FYM will provide up to 60 g per sq m (2 oz per sq yd) of nitrogen, 30 g per sq m (1 oz per sq yd) of phosphate, and 60 g per sq m (2 oz per sq yd) of potash, which is quite substantial compared with other organic materials. The same amount will also provide all the necessary trace elements for up to five years' cropping.

Garden compost The variety of ingredients used and their original condition means that garden compost is much more variable in content and in the time it takes to rot down than farmyard manure – that is where the difference ends. Well-made garden compost is just as good for the soil in every other way – moreover, to everyone with a garden it is free.

MAKING GARDEN COMPOST

Composting garden and household waste is quite simple as, left to its own devices, all plant and animal remains will eventually rot down. In the garden the idea is to speed up this process and, barring disasters, the end result is bound to be reasonable compost even if the waste is just piled up and left.

BASIC RULES

There are just six basic rules for making good garden compost:
● Enclose the area to make a tidy and manageable pile and always add a good depth of fresh material.
● Make the heap dimensions as big as practicable – 1 sq m (3 sq ft) is about the minimum practical size.
● Construct a container with materials having good insulation properties. Contrary to popular belief, if the compost heap is properly constructed inside the container, extra aeration, through or under its walls, is not required.
● Use any fresh or cooked plant or vegetable waste, but avoid hard woody waste unless you can shred it or smash it up with a hammer. To avoid attracting vermin do not include animal waste other than eggshells, and do not include newspapers unless they are used to provide some of the insulation.
● Mix the waste when it is added, especially if there are large quantities of one type, like lawn mowings or leaves. This will give an even blend of soft and hard, wet and dry, small and larger pieces. Mixing also keeps the heap well aerated, supplying oxygen to the micro-organisms responsible for composting.
● Cover the heap to keep out rain – water it when more moisture is required.

Following these rules will produce good

compost in six to nine months, depending on the time of the year and the temperature – cold weather prolongs the process considerably.

WEED-FREE COMPOST

There is nothing more annoying than an attractive, dark brown, crumbly layer of compost spread between vegetables turning into a forest of chickweed or annual meadow grass before your eyes. It is reasonably easy to keep a high proportion of weed seeds out of the heap by pulling out weeds from your beds and borders before they flower. To be on the safe side, remove weeds as soon as they appear. Lawn mowings may also have annual grass seeds in them – mowing more frequently should reduce the likelihood of these becoming a problem as well.

Keep out all perennial weeds – docks, dandelions, couch grass – unless they can be spread out in the sun for several days so you are quite sure they are dead and will not revive in the ideal conditions of the compost heap.

Dealing with any weed seeds that remain in the heap means cooking them to a temperature of at least 40°C (104°F) for two days or more. This can be achieved only by providing efficient insulation in a small heap; in a large heap the same effect is produced by its sheer size – about 1·8 m (6 ft) square and high appears adequate. In the latter case the outer layer, which provides the insulation, will not heat up enough. Chop it off at the end of the composting process and use it to start a new heap, using only the well rotted, weed-free centre of the heap in the garden.

MAKING THE HEAPS

Invariably, there is insufficient material from a small garden to construct a heap all in one go. Waste added a little at a time will be in a fair state of decomposition by the time the enclosure or bin is filled, without having heated greatly during the process (heating is an essential part of the decomposition process). To overcome this,

THREE PART COMPOST BIN

Where space permits, it is best to have a compost heap with three compartments: one for filling with recent waste; one for the compost in the process of decomposing; and the last for the compost ready for using in the garden. Forking the compost from one bin to another has the advantage of aerating it. The heap can be built on either soil or concrete.

it may be better to accumulate the waste separately and then mix and stack it in one operation when there is enough. The mixing adds extra air and restarts the composting process, giving a better end-product. Clearly, if you can spare the time and energy to turn and mix the heap even once after its first heating and cooling cycle it will pay dividends.

The ideal system is to have three 1·8 m (6 ft) square bins – constructed of wooden planks or lined with thick expanded polystyrene blocks for insulation – one filled, one to turn the freshly filled one into and allow it to mature, and a third for the mature compost currently being dug out for use.

Both experiment and experience have shown that there are no obvious benefits from constructing the heap on soil and no drawbacks to having it on solid surfaces, like brick or concrete, although asphalt seems to inhibit decay in the lower layers. Little benefit is derived from digging the soil beneath the heap, or from providing aeration at its base.

The heap should be sited in a shaded, sheltered spot.

ADDITIVES

In an evenly mixed heap it is unlikely that additives will speed up the process or make compost with better soil improving qualities. Watering on or mixing in a compost-maker or fertilizer is beneficial where large quantities of decay-resistant waste, like straw, prunings or evergreen leaves are included and mixing with the softer waste was not possible. The additives, of course, do increase the plant food value of the finished compost.

Nevertheless, although compost heaps regulate their own acidity producing roughly mature compost, in industrial areas it may be beneficial to use a compost maker, or to dust the surface of the heap with garden lime during its construction after every 15–23 cm (6–9 in) layer. This treatment is also a good idea if the waste is excessively wet or you find that the compost produced tends to be sticky or difficult to separate.

VEGETABLE GARDENING EQUIPMENT

There are several useful items which you should prepare in advance of the growing season. They will make your gardening much easier later on when you will be fully occupied sowing, planting, tending and harvesting your crops. None are particularly expensive to buy and some can be made simply.

SUPPORTS

Runner beans, climbing French beans and, to a lesser extent, peas are all popular crops which require some form of support.

PEA SUPPORTS

For the garden pea grower, twiggy sticks saved from hedge, tree and shrub prunings are traditional supports and still are considered to be the best way of controlling these sprawling plants (even the dwarf varieties tend to sprawl). Pea sticks are becoming more difficult to obtain, but several brands of durable, inexpensive plastic netting are available. When attached to canes or simple sticks pushed into the soil, they serve the same purpose most effectively.

Fencing in peas with a low wall of netting or polythene each side of a row can also be effective, but picking may be awkward. If using polythene, you should make sure a gap exists between the polythene and soil so there is plenty of air movement. Otherwise, mildew and botrytis (grey mould) may be a problem.

BEAN SUPPORTS

The main thing to remember about supporting runner beans is the weight of the plants and the wind resistance they offer when fully grown, particularly after heavy rain. Your bean poles – good bamboo

Twiggy pea sticks make the most attractive and effective support for peas, but they are becoming more and more difficult to obtain. Netting stretched between canes is a useful substitute.

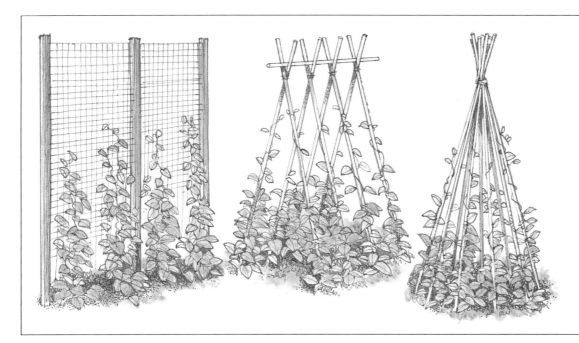

BEAN SUPPORTS
Stretch plastic netting across a wooden frame and have it free-standing. Otherwise, mount it against a wall.

Drive two rows of bamboo canes into the ground at a slight angle so they meet and cross near the top. Place poles in the V-channel and tie with string.

Arrange bamboo canes in a wigwam shape securing them at the top with string.

canes are best – must be well anchored in the soil and to each other.

The usual arrangement is to have double rows of poles about 23 cm (9 in) apart and 45 cm (18 in) between the rows, pushed at least 30 cm (12 in) into the soil – preferably more – at an angle so that the ends of the poles cross a short distance down from their tops (tie them together where they cross). Additional poles should be placed in the V-channel formed where the uprights cross, and also tied in position. To save on poles, stout strings can be substituted for some of them, but do make sure that you leave sufficient poles to provide good support for your crop.

Alternatively, the poles can be arranged in a wigwam shape, either tied at the top or pushed through flexible plastic discs specially designed for the job. Metal poles, rather like clothes-posts, to which strings or wires are attached to form a bell tent-like structure, are also available. These are easier to use and move, and take up much less space in the garden and when stored.

Improvised wooden frames with wire, string or plastic netting stretched across them can be used in various ways to support runner beans. Mount them vertically on walls and fences; in lean-to fashion against them; or they could be free-standing with supports. The strength of plastic netting is good enough for it to be used just suspended or supported between canes or poles in a single row.

A wooden frame is more expensive than an aluminium frame, but is better at conserving heat. The glass lights usually slide open on runners, making it easy to regulate the ventilation.

CLOCHES

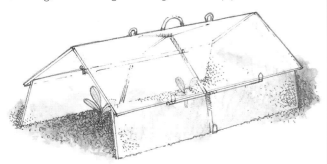

A plastic tunnel cloche, made with wire hoops and plastic sheeting, covers a large area of ground cheaply.

A barn cloche, made from panes of glass held together by a wire frame, is costly but excellent for large plants.

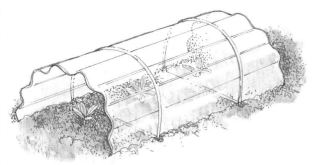

A corrugated PVC cloche, held in position with wire hoops, is long-lasting, and serves many uses. Being light, it is easy to move.

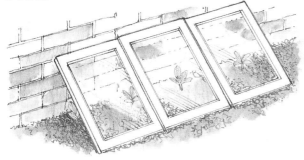

An improvised cloche, made by leaning some spare window panes against a wall.

Two different types of frame: the kind in the centre of the picture is made from corrugated PVC secured by wire hoops; the nearer one consists of panes of glass held in wire frames. When the plants inside are sufficiently sturdy to withstand the cold, the frames can be removed.

TRANSPARENT PROTECTION

Lights (the detachable lid of a frame) and cloches made from glass or acrylic, polycarbonate or polythene sheet are useful for protecting seedlings and plants from cold and wet. They also give a much longer growing season and, therefore, enable you to grow earlier and later crops outdoors.

Cloches are also useful for hardening off. This is when seedlings which were germinated indoors are placed in a frame and gradually exposed more and more to outdoor temperatures before being finally transplanted to the plot. To harden off plants, remove the cloches from each row in the daytime when the weather is not too cold; replace them in the evening.

When propped against walls and fences, several pairs of frames can be used together to form a row of large cloches over early broad beans or salad crops, like winter lettuces. Smaller pieces of the rigid

Tent-like cloches, made from rigid glazing materials and secured at the top with strong clips. This type of cloche, which is easily assembled, has the advantage of being compact to store.

glazing materials can also be made into instant tent-like cloches with the help of wire frames.

You can also make polythene sheeting into tunnel cloches with the aid of wire hoops and string. The hoops can be bought ready-made, but soft galvanized wire is easily bent to form them or, even cheaper, use the wire clothes hangers from dry-cleaners. Remember, too, that mini-cloches can be fashioned from the multitude of transparent plastic containers that are given away – giant lemonade bottles and jerry cans, to name just two. The advantage of plastic cloches is that the larger ones are easier to carry than the glass ones of equivalent size. You can grow up to two or three rows of vegetables

to maturity in the larger ones. Heavy-duty polythene will last for up to three or four years. Take into account, as well, the size of crops you will be growing before choosing your cloche. As a general rule of thumb, choose a cloche which is approximately twice as high and one-and-a-half times as wide as the nearly matured vegetables. Clean the glass, polythene or plastic when it gets dirty, in order to continue to allow light in.

You do not need to remove cloches before you water vegetables or fruit. Simply water on top of the cloche, and the water will run down the sides and into the soil beside the plants. Watch for sudden changes in weather. On warm days, open up cloches to keep the temperature down.

Close them again about an hour before nightfall. On frosty nights, cover the cloches with sheets of newspaper.

Breakages add to the cost of using glass cloches. Bear in mind, however, that transparent plastic materials, particularly polythene sheeting, do not have the same heat-retention properties as glass – under plastic cloches with their ends on, for example, the temperature can be lower than that found outside. Also, because humidity tends to be higher inside than out, and as wet cold is more damaging to plants than dry cold, it is advisable to provide some ventilation to correct this situation, and to prevent the onset of the fungal diseases which are likely to develop rapidly in humid conditions.

MANAGING THE PLOT

Growing vegetables successfully depends on a range of factors: making the best use of your ground, knowing when to sow and plant, when to feed and water, and so on, but first you must decide what to grow.

PLANNING WHAT TO GROW

Putting on paper your crop preferences and making notes on the timing of the various operations will help you to formulate an overall plan.

A mixture of staple and favourite vegetables is most likely to be your starting point. It pays to be a little over-cautious at first, until the mysteries and benefits of successional sowing, catch cropping, intercropping, intersowing, close spacing, optimum spacing and bed systems are all revealed (see pages 22 to 25).

Keep your plan simple and first learn how to become efficient at growing just a few crops. Try not to be tempted into growing crops or varieties of dubious reliability or hardiness in your part of the country.

In cold years, outdoor cucumbers, tomatoes, probably sweetcorn and even kidney and runner beans can be disappointing. So it's a good idea to look at established vegetable plots in your vicinity, see which crops are being grown, and ask your neighbours and local allotment gardeners to recommend varieties they have found to be reliable.

In recent years plant breeders have been putting great efforts into developing earlier, more hardy varieties for growing from seed. Together with your own observations and the knowledge of local gardeners, these varieties will almost guarantee a good crop wherever you live.

The availability of a freezer, and space or facilities for storing onions and root vegetables will influence your plan, as will the price of vegetables in the shops. Winter brassicas, for instance, can be expensive and may be well worth growing for their economic value. Since other crops

A well planned plot in which every available space is occupied by healthy vegetables.

will have to be omitted to make room for such a crop, the plan may have to be amended. This, in turn, may make it more difficult to give a roughly equal area of ground to the three main types of vegetables – the cabbage family, the root crops and the legumes (peas and beans), plus the remaining crops. The significance of this is covered in the section on crop rotation (see pages 25 to 28).

In order to take account of these many factors, your plan will need to be flexible.

The A–Z of Vegetables chapter, which gives approximate sowing dates, planting-out times and the length of time the crop is in the ground before harvesting, will be helpful.

MAXIMIZING YOUR CROPS

Ways to increase the quantity of vegetables which can be harvested from the same amount of ground have always been sought by gardeners. One method is to

VEGETABLE GARDENING

SUCCESSIONAL SOWING
Sow quick growing crops, like lettuces, at frequent intervals to give you a steady supply of fresh produce.

CATCH CROPPING
As the broccoli and cauliflower are harvested, the ground they occupied is used for quick growing crops.

protect seeds, seedlings and young plants with cloches and cold frames, or to raise seed in a greenhouse or on a windowsill before planting out in more clement conditions. In this way the growing season is extended, thus increasing the crop.

Making the best possible use of the ground available is another way.

ORNAMENTAL VEGETABLES
In small gardens, where lack of space may prevent you setting aside a plot solely for vegetables, it's worth considering growing ornamental crops in flower borders.

With their scarlet flowers and climbing habit, runner beans look most effective trained up a wall or even over an arch or pergola. A row of sweet corn makes an attractive windbreak and fennel is a wonderful foliage backdrop.

SUCCESSIONAL SOWING
It makes sense to sow quick growing crops, such as radishes, and vegetables that do not keep well, at frequent intervals during the year so that there is always a fresh crop coming on. Successional sowing, as it is called, can be applied to beetroot, carrots, lettuce, spring onions, spinach and even dwarf beans. Two or three sowings of dwarf beans – one under cloches in March or April, one at the usual May/June time and one during July – will provide pickings well into autumn, especially under cloches. Sow only short rows of the salad types, about 1 m (3 ft) at a time.

Sweet corn makes an effective and decorative windbreak in this garden, where vegetables and pretty flowering annuals grow side by side.

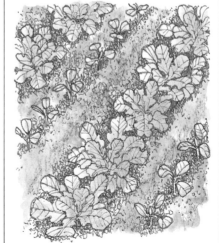

INTERCROPPING
While long-term crops are still young, use the ground in between for quick growing crops.

Notice how the space left between the runner bean poles has been filled with 'Salad Bowl' lettuces. These particular varieties have great ornamental value, as the leaves are picked off the plants, just a few at a time – the plants remain in the ground until the end of the season.

CATCH CROPPING

Whenever an area of soil becomes vacant between crops, or even when a single plant or row fails unexpectedly, put in a catch crop. Any of those vegetables used for successional sowing will usually be satisfactory, perhaps with the exception of dwarf beans which may take a little too long, although in the broccoli plot they would be an ideal catch crop from the end of May onwards.

INTERCROPPING

The same principle as catch cropping applies, but this method makes use of the soil between rows of long-term crops, like Brussels sprouts, before they get too big and spread out across the rows, cutting off the light from the soil below. It can be used for growing salad crops or for raising seedlings of other brassicas for transplanting later.

When the maincrop plants are young and there appear to be acres of bare soil between the rows, it is all too easy to be over enthusiastic with intercropping. Beware of ending up with a shorter crop which is planted too thickly, swamped by the maincrop which deprives it of light and air, and makes it impossible to get between the plants to weed, spray, or pick.

A row of lettuces has been planted in between these runner beans to make use of available space and light, before the beans grow taller – a practice known as catch cropping.

23

VEGETABLE GARDENING

With extra plants competing for light, water and food in such a limited area, thorough watering and liquid feeding or dry top dressing will be necessary.

INTERSOWING

Mixing two or more types of seed for sowing in the same row is a useful technique. It makes more efficient use of the plot, and also has other advantages. Using a quick germinator, like radishes, which marks out the row quickly and clearly, with a slower germinator, like parsnips, makes hoeing down the row much easier. The quick-growing crop will be picked long before the maincrop needs the space.

Sowing spring onions with carrots is another possibility. Though not conclusively proven, there is some evidence that the onion smell disguises the carrot smell (especially when the onions are being thinned or pulled) which confuses the carrot fly in its search for carrots.

Vegetables with varieties which mature at different times are other possible candidates for intersowing. Lettuce is the usual crop for this treatment, but seed of mixed varieties of Brussels sprouts and courgettes is also available now.

CLOSE SPACING

Growing plants more closely together than recommended can be beneficial in crops like carrots, where regular thinnings are made as the roots begin to swell for use as an early, tender vegetable. Closer spacing between rows, or double planting (using two rows together with a pathway between every pair) also make more intensive use of space.

The carrots here have been sown closer together than usual to take up less room in the vegetable plot.

OPTIMUM SPACING

The normal way of planting vegetables in rows with even spacing between the plants is not an efficient use of space. The open soil on each side of the plants initially provides more air, light, water and nutrients but as weeds have no competition they rapidly take over. The gaps between the plants in the row are then filled with weeds which compete with the vegetables. The crop plants become uneven in size and any irregularity in planting distances increases this unevenness yet further.

Optimum spacing – the answer to this – is one of the most fundamental changes in vegetable-growing thinking in recent years. This is actually equidistant spacing but, as all crops have a different maximum size at maturity, each will require a different growing space. The idea is that when a plant is fully grown its leaves will just touch its neighbours on all sides. In theory, this means growing each plant in an imaginary circle, but in practice it simply involves having staggered rows.

BED SYSTEMS

The optimum spacing system is best used in blocks since rows, even double rows,

CLOSE SPACING
When carrots are sown close together, the thinnings can be used in cooking.

must give some degree of variation on their outer, unprotected sides. Using quite narrow beds, 1·2 m (4 ft) or 1·5 m (5 ft) across, with paths between, and growing short rows of vegetables across their width, allows access from both sides of the bed. This gives optimum spacing and growing conditions for all the crops and largely prevents weeds by excluding

INTERSOWING
Mix and then sow two or more types of seed together in the same row. Onions and carrots combined reduce the risk of carrot fly.

The bed system divides a plot up into small square or rectangular beds with paths in between.

OPTIMUM SPACING
When vegetables are grown in unstaggered rows, they take up more space, and also develop unevenly.

When vegetables are planted in staggered rows, they take up less room, and the light they receive is regular, so they develop well.

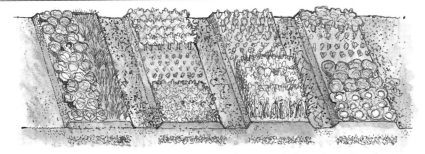

A BED SYSTEM
A bed system consists of a series of small beds, no more than 1·2–1·5 m (4–5 ft) wide, with narrow paths in between. It should be possible to always work from the paths, thus avoiding treading on the cultivated soil and damaging its soil structure. Optimum spacing (see above) makes best use of the ground available.

light from the soil between the plants. A further advantage of this system is that there is no need to walk on the beds, even when sowing and planting, so the damage caused to the soil structure when wet soil is walked upon doesn't occur.

From this a refinement has developed – the 'deep-bed system' – in which the beds are double dug, the soil in the bottom spit thoroughly enriched with organic manure and the topsoil kept loose and open to form a slightly raised bed. In very wet or cold areas a bed can be as much as 15–20 cm (6–8 in) above the pathways to aid drainage and encourage the soil to warm more quickly in the spring.

Bed systems lend themselves well to covering with 'floating cloches' – clear, perforated polythene sheeting laid over the seed bed or seedlings which are then able to grow underneath, protected but without hindrance. Covering the soil with black polythene sheeting will keep the soil drier and warms it up even earlier.

CROP ROTATION

Vegetables that grow in the same way (for the groupings see the chart on page 27) tend to be attacked by groups of pests and diseases. To prevent the build-up and

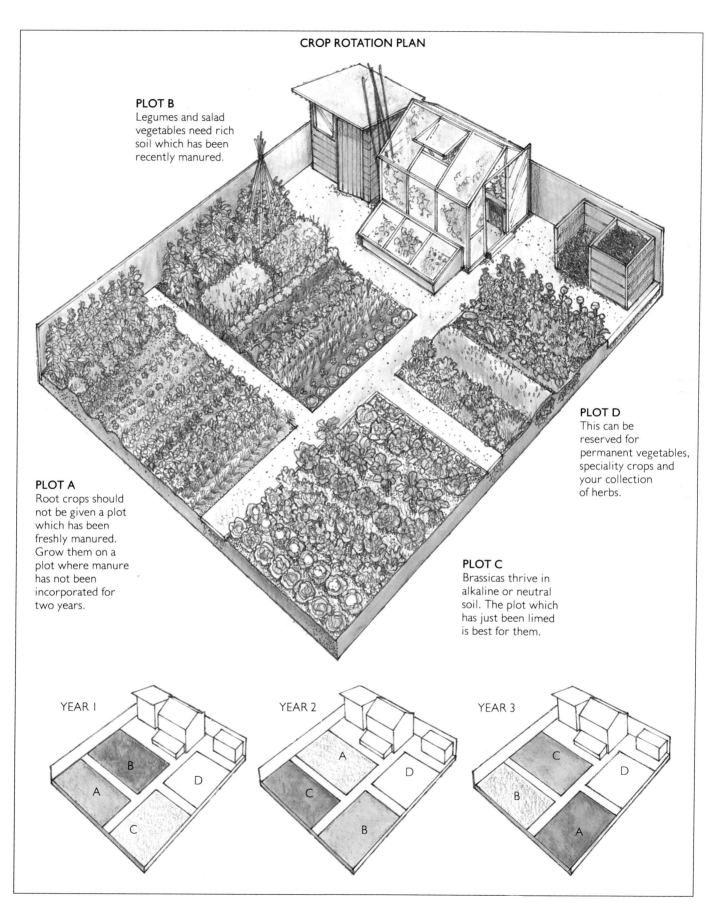

CROP ROTATION PLAN

PLOT B
Legumes and salad vegetables need rich soil which has been recently manured.

PLOT D
This can be reserved for permanent vegetables, speciality crops and your collection of herbs.

PLOT A
Root crops should not be given a plot which has been freshly manured. Grow them on a plot where manure has not been incorporated for two years.

PLOT C
Brassicas thrive in alkaline or neutral soil. The plot which has just been limed is best for them.

YEAR I

YEAR 2

YEAR 3

transfer of pests and diseases attracted to a particular type of plant, it would help to grow all vegetables on fresh soil every year. On smaller plots this is impossible, so a system was devised to ensure that crops are grown on the same ground as infrequently as possible.

Dividing the area available into sections and growing a different group on each area every year – 'rotating' them – is the solution. The Victorians used a seven-year rotation but nowadays, when gardens and allotments are much smaller, the three-year rotation is virtually the only system widely used.

Unfortunately, moving crops a few yards from year to year will not deter above-ground pests to any great extent, except where other preventative measures are taken (see the chapter on Pests and Diseases). Below-ground pests, also, will only be deterred if they are specific to one

Above: Legumes like peas and beans should be grown in rich soil where plenty of manure has been incorporated.

Right: Root crops such as carrots should not be grown on freshly manured soil.

particular crop and move about in the soil very little, like the minute eelworms which affect potatoes and cabbages.

The occurrence of plant diseases (most of which are caused by fungus attacks), however, is reduced by crop rotation. Fungi grow from minute spores, ever present in the air and soil. Dividing the plot into three roughly equal areas and

allowing a gap of at least two years before growing the same group of crops on the same soil is therefore an extremely worthwhile measure.

The order in which the vegetable groups follow each other on the same soil is important because, although the main benefit is disease control, the regular additions of fertilizers contribute greatly to soil

VEGETABLE GROUPS FOR CROP ROTATION			
Root crops	Brassicas	Legumes and salad vegetables	Permanent and specialist vegetables
beetroot carrot chicory Jerusalem artichoke parsnip potato swede turnip	broccoli Brussels sprout cabbage calabrese cauliflower kale kohl rabi radish	asparagus pea beans, broad, kidney and runner celeriac celery endive leek lettuce onion and shallot pea spinach, spinach beet and leaf beet sweet corn	asparagus aubergine capsicum cucumber Florence fennel globe artichoke herbs marrow, courgette, pumpkin and squash tomato

fertility. Legumes (peas and beans), onions, beet and salad crops need plenty of rich manure so this is dug in for them. Root crops, however, must not have fresh manure so they are kept away from the manured section, arriving there two years after it has been manured, by which time the manure has largely rotted away leaving only a fertile residue of humus.

PLANTS, SEEDS, SEED BEDS AND SOWING

PLANTS

Always buy vegetable plants from a reliable source. You can then be sure that the plants have been grown from seed in clean, sterile compost. The cabbages will not start with club root and will have been protected from cabbage rootfly attack; tomatoes and cucumbers will not be affected by viruses. Also, all the plants will be correctly labelled.

The best plant sources will insist on these rules being stringently observed by their suppliers and they will only sell the plants at the right time of the year. It is no use, for example, having marrow plants on display in April when they should not be planted out until June. You should be able to plant your specimens in the garden soon after buying them, so make sure that you can cope with the quantities you buy.

Generally, good clean, green and healthy plants are their own advertisement. Always avoid plants with yellowing, eaten or mildew-powdered leaves. The compost should be evenly moist and not shrunken away from the sides of the

Left: Brassicas prefer neutral or slightly alkaline conditions. Grow them on a plot which has just been limed.

Florence fennel can be grown in the fourth bed of a rotation scheme.

pot or tray, and large roots should not be protruding from the bottom of the container, a sign of starvation. You can carefully tap out pot-grown plants to examine the root system, which should be white. If a plant is healthy and not pot bound or too old, some unused compost should be showing between the roots.

SEEDS

Growing vegetables from seed is still the most popular way and, for most kinds, the only possible method. It is also cheaper than buying plants, and raising them under controlled conditions will ensure a healthy stock.

Although vegetable seeds must comply with extremely strict laws on reliability of germination, cleanliness and purity, they can still vary considerably, depending on their source and how they were treated since harvesting. There is no point in

skimping – for good crops you must buy the best quality seed, preferably sold in air-tight foil envelopes; these can help keep them fresher for much longer.

Pelleted seeds are single seeds coated in a soft, dry clay, which makes the tiny ones easier to sow individually. The work of thinning and transplanting is greatly reduced and there is less waste, but it is still advisable to sow two or three pellets at each position in case some do not germinate. Pelleted seed is, of course, more expensive and thorough watering is essential to ensure that the coating is dissolved, allowing the seed to take up water for its germination.

What used to be referred to as a seed variety – indicating some variation and advantage over other varieties of the same crop – is now often called a cultivar, the term being derived from the words 'cultivated variety'. This means that the

Vegetable seeds raised in trays or pots should be sown in the best John Innes seed compost. Make sure it is free of lumps.

variety has been specifically chosen or bred for garden cultivation.

'F1' cultivars are varieties that have been bred for a particular set of qualities, such as early cropping, sweet flavour, or even – in the case of the pea 'Bikini' – almost leaflessness. The qualities are selected in parent plants and pure lines of these are bred through many generations before they are finally crossed or mated with each other to produce the F1 seed. This is extremely pure, resulting in plants which are almost identical and which produce uniform, and usually much heavier, crops. Obviously, this expertise has to be paid for, so F1 seed is relatively expensive. Its reliability usually makes up for this, however, and its more precise cropping period makes the produce ideal for storing in the deep freeze.

Seed beds and sowing Whether you are sowing in boxes, pots or the open ground, the ideal conditions are the same – the soil must have a fine, crumb-like consistency, a firm level surface and be evenly moist, but not wet.

In a seed tray or pot this is achieved by using the best John Innes seed compost or a peat-based compost, which will be free of lumps. Over-fill the seed tray or pot and

PRICKING OUT SEEDLINGS

1. When the young seedlings are large enough to handle, loosen their roots with a stick, and prick them out holding by the leaf, not the stem.

2. Fill new trays with John Innes potting compost No. 1 and, making holes large enough to take the seedling roots, plant them up to their necks.

3. Place a fine rose on the watering can and gently water in the seedlings. Make sure that you keep them out of direct sunlight for a few days.

carefully push the compost into the corners before levelling off and firming with a flat piece of wood to about 6 mm ($\frac{1}{4}$ in) below the rim.

Outdoors, if you dig medium to heavy soils in winter, leaving rough clods, you will get a 'frost mould' or finely crumbled surface by spring. Don't walk on this when it is wet, but once it is dry enough not to stick to your boots, firming with your heels and raking to a fine tilth (often described as wheat-sized grains of soil) will produce an ideal seed bed.

Lighter soils usually dry out more quickly and can be dug in spring, but the seed bed is made in the same way. Covering any soil with cloches or polythene (see pages 19 to 20) will warm it and dry it quickly for an earlier start.

Approximate sowing depths and distances for each crop are given in the A–Z of Vegetables chapter, but the general rules are:

● Sow at the right time. A little variation, to make allowances for the weather and growing conditions, will always be necessary, but try to resist sowing too early – this is one of the commonest causes of failure.

● Sow at the right depth. Many seeds will not germinate if they are sown too deeply or the soil is firmed over them too severely, especially if it is cold and wet.

● Sow thinly. Sowing too many seeds is wasteful and means that more time is needed for thinning out and tending the seedlings. They will also be more prone to collapsing from damping-off or other plant diseases.

These rules apply to seeds in trays, pots and in the open soil, but the sowing techniques vary. In trays and pots, covering smaller seeds with a shallow layer of moist vermiculite is, perhaps, an easier method than using a precise depth of sifted seed compost. In the case of tomatoes, though, sharp sand is better because it helps to remove any sticky seed coats as the tiny seedlings emerge.

On the plot, sowing in drills (shallow grooves) made with a hoe, the back of a rake or even a stick, is still the most common method, even where a bed system is being used. Use a garden line (low-priced polypropylene string will last indefinitely) to make straight, neat rows. If the string is stretched and the end stake pushed in at an angle away from the end of

SOWING SEED OUTDOORS

1. Rake ground which was previously dug over, working it to a fine tilth. If necessary, add a base dressing (see page 11) at the same time.

2. Stretch a line down the rows and make straight, shallow drills or grooves, using a pointed stick or a draw hoe.

3. Water the drill lightly. Sow the seeds as evenly and thinly as possible to prevent wastage and reduce the need for thinning out later on.

4. Cover the seeds by shuffling along the rows, pushing the soil back over the drill. Write labels to indicate crop name and sowing date.

Sow the seed in shallow grooves, taking care not to scatter it too deeply.

VEGETABLE SOWING CALENDAR

VEGETABLE	SITE	TIME	VEGETABLE	SITE	TIME

ASPARAGUS	outdoors	April	ENDIVE,
			  curly
			  Batavian
				outdoors
				outdoors
					March–Aug
					July–Sept

ASPARAGUS PEA	under glass outdoors	early April May	FLORENCE FENNEL	outdoors	April
AUBERGINE	peat pots under glass	March			
BEANS, BROAD	cloche outdoors outdoors, mild areas	Jan–March Feb–May Oct–Dec	KALE	outdoors	April–May
			KOHL RABI	outdoors	April–Aug
BEANS, KIDNEY	under glass outdoors	Mar–April May–July	LEEK	under glass outdoors	Feb–March March–early June
BEANS, RUNNER	under glass outdoors	mid Mar–April mid May–July	LETTUCE	under glass outdoors	Feb–March March–Aug

BEETROOT	peat pots under glass
	  or cloches
	outdoors
		late Feb
		early April–July
			MARROW,
			  COURGETTE,
			  PUMPKIN,
			  SQUASH
				under glass
				outdoors
					April
					early June

BROCCOLI	outdoors	April–May	ONION, SHALLOT	under glass outdoors	Dec–Jan Feb–March or Aug
BRUSSELS SPROUTS	under glass outdoors	late Feb–early March mid March–April	PARSNIP	outdoors	late Feb–April

CABBAGE,
  spring
  summer
 	
  winter
  savoy
	outdoors
	under glass
	outdoors
	outdoors
	outdoors
		July–Aug
		Feb–March
		March–early May
		April–May
		April–May
			PEAS	cloches in mild areas
				cloches in cold areas
				outdoors
					Oct–Nov
					Feb–March
					April–June

CALABRESE	outdoors	April–July	RADISH,
			  summer
			
			  winter
				cloches
				outdoors
				
				outdoors
					Jan–Feb
					March–May and
					  Aug–Sept
					July–Aug

CAPSICUM	peat pots under glass	March			

CARROTS,
  short
 	
  intermediate
  and long
	cloches
	outdoors
	
	outdoors
		Feb–March
		March–July
		
		April–June
			SPINACH,
			  summer
			  winter
			  New Zealand
			  leaf beet
				outdoors
				outdoors
				outdoors
				outdoors
					March–May
					Aug–Sept
					May
					April

CAULIFLOWER	outdoors	mid March–May	SWEDE	outdoors	April–June
CELERIAC	peat pots under glass	Feb–March	SWEETCORN	peat pots under glass outdoors	April June
CELERY	under glass	Mar–April	TOMATO	under glass	April

CHICORY,
  forcing
  non-forcing
	outdoors
	outdoors
		May–June
		June–July
			TURNIP,
			  earlies
			
			  spring greens
				cloches
				outdoors
				outdoors
					Feb
					March–April
					July–Aug

CUCUMBER	peat pots under glass	April			

the row, it will remain taut when the drill is drawn.

After sowing the seed, shuffle along the row, using your feet to push in the soil and cover the seeds from each side. Or use a rake – always from the side, never along the row, otherwise all the seed could finish up at one end of the plot.

Fluid drilling, a new technique, sometimes used by commercial vegetable growers, is worthy of mention. This involves sowing pre-germinated seed. Sow ordinary seed from a packet on moist tissue paper, taking care not to flood it and keep at the temperature recommended for germination on the packet. When the majority of seeds have just produced their first shoot or root, carefully mix them with thin wallpaper paste (one without a fungicide) in a large polythene bag. Once the seed drill is prepared, cut off a small bottom corner of the bag and squeeze out the seedling/paste mixture, as if icing a cake, along the drill. Cover with soil and tend the crop as usual. With fluid drilling it is important to observe the normal seed-sowing timing – the pre-germinated seedlings are very tender and adverse weather conditions can give them an even greater set-back if you are not careful.

Hoe between the rows of vegetables to keep weeds down – catch the weeds when they are still seedlings.

WEEDING

Like all plants, weeds need space, air, light, food and water. They will deprive the vegetables of this, so reducing the potential harvest. They will also harbour pests and diseases.

There are many types of weeds in the garden but, for the purposes of getting rid of them, they can be divided into two groups. Annuals are plants which grow, flower and seed at least once in a year; while perennials keep going for many years.

The distinctions between the two different groups are important because they determine the way in which the weeds are treated and controlled.

HOEING

Among growing vegetables, annuals and small seedlings, perennial weeds are best removed by hand or by hoeing. Hoeing has the additional advantage of loosening the soil surface to form a weed-free, moisture-retentive layer or mulch. Hoe only during dry weather so that the uprooted and decapitated weeds shrivel and die before they get a chance to re-root. Use a hoe which is suited both to the job in question and your personal requirements – your height and strength for example.

Onion hoe This is suitable for delicate work amongst seedlings. It keeps the soil loose and open and the surface dry, discouraging further weed seeds from germinating and preventing the evaporation of valuable water from the ground by acting as a mulch.

Draw hoe As its name suggests, the draw hoe is drawn towards the gardener, cutting off the weeds with its backward facing edge. This action makes it easy to avoid the plants.

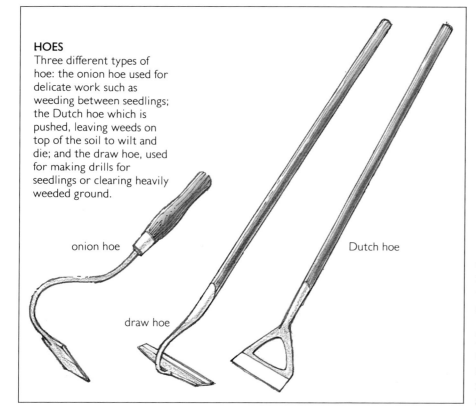

HOES
Three different types of hoe: the onion hoe used for delicate work such as weeding between seedlings; the Dutch hoe which is pushed, leaving weeds on top of the soil to wilt and die; and the draw hoe, used for making drills for seedlings or clearing heavily weeded ground.

onion hoe

draw hoe

Dutch hoe

Dutch hoe This is often D-shaped, with the cutting edge on the straight bar; it is pushed away from the user. It is easier to damage plants with this type if you're not careful, but it has the advantage of being much easier on the back and arms.

When choosing either the Dutch or the draw hoe, make certain that the handle is long enough; it needs to reach at least the shoulder when it being used at the correct angle. Also make sure that the blade is at the right angle to the shaft: in use it should be almost parallel to the ground. Finally, keep the cutting edge sharp by frequently filing it or using a sharpening stone. Hoes, like all gardening tools, should be cleaned and wiped over with an oily rag before putting them away.

STALE SEED BED METHOD
Launching an attack on annual and perennial weeds before they even appear is the essence of the 'stale seed bed' method, most valuable for the clean start it gives. After preparing the seed bed, it is left for some days until the majority of the weed seeds disturbed or exposed by the digging and preparation have germinated and emerged as seedlings. These are then burnt off, either with a paraffin-fired flame gun, or chemically with a contact weedkiller like paraquat. With a little luck and by making an effort to disturb the bed as infrequently as possible afterwards, the soil can often remain free of weeds for almost the whole season.

DIGGING
Perennial weeds, like bindweed, ground elder and dandelion or the narrow-leaved couch grass, must be thoroughly removed when digging as they all have the ability to sprout and grow again from the tiniest piece of root left in the ground. Just hoeing off their tops is ineffective.

Turning young annual weeds into the bottom of the trench when digging is effective if you can be absolutely certain that there are no perennials larger than seedlings present.

MULCHING
As mentioned previously, loosening the soil surface when hoeing forms a weed-free moisture-retentive layer or mulch. Covering the soil with another layer of material will have the same effect and give extra benefits like reducing weed growth.

A good mulch should be thick enough to prevent weed seeds germinating and stop water evaporating from the soil, while allowing rain or irrigation water through without hindrance. Rotted manure, garden compost, peat or spent mushroom compost are much the best materials: a 5 cm (2 in) layer effectively prevents many weed seeds from germinating, but also makes any perennial weeds that come through a great deal easier to pull out. It also encourages worms, whose soil-moving activities aerate the soil and slowly decay the organic mulch, to add humus and trace elements to it.

WEEDKILLERS
It is important to understand the effects of various weedkillers before applying them.

Contact weedkillers, like paraquat, kill the green parts of all types of plants above the ground. They are useful for clearing ground of annual weeds before sowing or planting.

Residual weedkillers, like simazine, are applied to the soil and prevent weed seeds from germinating and young seedlings from growing.

Translocated weedkillers are taken up by the leaves and roots to kill the whole plant. They are used for clearing land of established perennials when making a new vegetable plot, or for specific kinds of weed problem, like bindweed in the sweetcorn, or grass weeds in the cabbage patch. The most useful types, they are further divided into three groups according to the plants they kill.

Total weedkillers, like glyphosphate, which kill virtually all annual and perennial, broad-leaved and grass-type weeds.
Broad-leaved weedkillers, like '2, 4D' which kill only dicotyledons (non-grass weeds).
Grass weedkillers, like alloxydim sodium, which kill some annual grasses but mainly persistent perennial species, especially couch grass (*Agropyron repens*), a particularly stubborn weed.

Applying weedkillers Always use weedkillers carefully. They are not as poisonous these days, compared with the arsenic and mercury compounds used in the past, but they are still dangerous, especially in concentrated form.

Keep clearly marked, separate sprayers from watering cans, and apply only in still, cool weather. Drifting spray can cause severe damage in the garden, and in warm weather the vapour, even from a lawn weedkiller being used some distance away, can affect plants: tomatoes for instance acquire an unpleasant taste resembling disinfectant.

A layer of thick black polythene acts as an effective mulch for preventing loss of moisture from the soil in summer.

FEEDING

The original organic manure, lime and fertilizer base dressing used on the plot to recondition impoverished soil, to prepare for planting and to feed the crops as they become established (see pages 10 to 15), will not be sufficient for most vegetables for a whole season. The soil will not be impoverished and the plants will not starve, but there is a point at which insufficient plant nutrients are available to produce the best crop in quality or quantity. So, after some weeks (exact timing depends on the vegetable), the crop will need extra feeding in the form of a top dressing.

The same fertilizer given as a base dressing may be used, but liquid feeding with a fortified seaweed or a soluble plant food will give the most efficient and quickest response. The easy-to-remember rule is to use as much solution, at the recommended strength, as you would for a thorough watering. This could be as little as 300 ml ($\frac{1}{2}$ pint) for young tomato plants or as much as 9 litres (2 gallons) for plants heavy with several trusses of fruit. The beauty of this simple feeding rule is that it does away with the complicated instructions necessary to cater for every stage of every crop in different soils, in differing climates, and at varying times of the year.

Where there is a variation from this rule or additional feeding is considered to be

FEEDING METHODS

When only small amounts of liquid feed are required for a crop, it is simplest to dilute the plant food in the watering can, and then pour it around the base of the plants.

For large volumes of liquid feed, use a hose-end dilutor. Place a special fertilizer block in the dissolver canister attached to the end of the hose pipe.

important, it is noted under the individual crop in the chapter on A–Z of Vegetables.

Large volumes of liquid feed take a surprisingly long time to water on and a hose-end dilutor, which uses water directly from the tap to dilute a concentrated solution, makes the task much easier. There are small 568 ml (1 pint) or 1136 ml (2 pint)-bottle versions, but take care to select one that produces a large volume of coarse spray which will apply enough liquid to feed all the plants adequately and in a reasonable time as well.

Do not choose the fine-spray types,

suitable for pesticides or foliar feeding, because they do not apply a large enough volume to root-feed efficiently. There is a large-volume coarse-spray type which attaches to a watering can rather than a small bottle and therefore has the added advantage of supplying a lot more liquid feed from just one filling of the concentrate, so consider one of these.

WATERING

In the majority of years, even the wettest ones, there is almost invariably a time when the soil becomes too dry to give the best possible crop. Leaving watering until the soil becomes noticeably dry will not only reduce the quantity but also the quality of the crop by inducing woodiness in carrots and beets, and toughness in beans. Also, as roots and fruits suddenly find themselves with abundant water after a period of drought, they expand and may eventually split.

Digging in plenty of organic manure on plots other than those with root vegetables (see Crop rotation pages 25 to 28), and mulching in spring, after the wettest part of the year, will conserve water, but more will almost certainly be needed.

HOW MUCH WATER?

Water thoroughly and carefully. It is most important to give enough to suit the crop and the circumstances. Soil loses water by evaporation and plants literally suck it out, to the extent that 1 sq m (1 sq yd) of

Digging plenty of well rotted manure into the soil will help conserve water, thus reducing your summer tasks.

ground may lose up to 20 litres (4½ gallons) in just one week of dry weather. There is, therefore, no point in just sprinkling water around plants. It will do little good and could be harmful, inducing plants to make roots close to the soil's surface in an attempt to get at the small amount of water available. The resulting roots will then be even more susceptible to drought as evaporation dries out the soil on the surface.

For overall watering never use less than 5 litres per sq m (1 gallon per sq yd) and preferably 10 litres per sq m (2 gallons per sq yd). Seedlings may need less volume at each watering, but it will be required more often. Because the plants develop rapidly and use more and more water, the total amount applied for seedlings may well be the same.

WATERING METHODS

In larger vegetable gardens a hosepipe is all but essential in dry weather. Turning down the flow to a trickle for careful watering alongside each plant is the ideal way of watering seedlings and young transplants until they are sturdier and better able to withstand overhead watering by hand or automatic sprinkler.

Measuring the amount of water applied is simple with the various types of overhead sprinkler, using a row of jars or tins across the width of the spray. These will indicate when 2·5 cm (1 in) of water has been applied, as well as showing clearly any variation over the area so that the sprinkler can be moved to compensate.

You can also measure the amount of water applied by using a perforated flat hose. This gives an ultra-fine upward spray, although it will naturally take a lot longer. The 'weeping' or 'seeping' type of hose, however, is made of porous plastic or it has a stitched row of perforations down the edge which allows water just to seep or drip out. Consequently, these kinds will moisten soil directly. To calculate the amount they have used, the flow rate from the tap must be multiplied by the length of time they are left running. These are the gentlest of all and are unlikely to cause any damage to the plants or soil unless left on for a very long time.

Finally, there are hose-end dilutors. These can be used for feeding and for watering (see page 11), applying water at the same time as the root and foliar feed.

HARVESTING

One of the most important reasons for growing your own vegetables is that they can be enjoyed at the peak of perfection. Precisely when this is will depend on a number of things. Not all vegetables are harvested when they are ripe. Beetroot, for instance, are delectable when young and no bigger than a golf ball, so they need not all be grown on as a main crop and pickled or stored for the winter. Carrots are another example: sowing them more thickly than recommended will provide a succulent crop of tender young roots, thinner than a finger, which have a distinctly different, but equally pleasant flavour compared with their mature roots.

Courgettes are only small marrows: at that stage they are quite different from the mature vegetable and picking them encourages more to develop, with the result that you can have courgettes followed by marrows. Cut the courgettes when they are no longer than 7·5–10 cm (3–4 in).

Beans need to be picked relatively young if the pods are not to become tough or stringy – unless, of course, the dried seed is wanted for red kidney or haricot beans to be used through the winter.

Some vegetables must be grown on until mature or they will not keep: marrows and the large onions are examples, although there is nothing to stop you picking or pulling any crops for immediate use throughout the summer.

For details on when and how to harvest specific vegetables see the A–Z of Vegetables chapter.

HOW TO HARVEST

There are several points to bear in mind when harvesting your crops:
- They must be firm, thoroughly ripened, well dried and free from rots or other plant diseases.
- With root vegetables, take great care in lifting the below-ground parts. The underground spread of many crops grows deeply and is not easy to see, and they are all too easily speared. Keep the fork well back from the line of the leaves to avoid damaging them and causing consequent rotting in store.
- Do not damage either the vegetables themselves or the plants from which they are picked. Do not tear peas or beans from their vines, since stems damaged in this way seldom recover fully. Cut the leaves of leaf crops cleanly wherever possible – beetroot leaves, however, should be twisted off.
- A few vegetables do not deteriorate with age – within reason, of course. Jerusalem artichokes can be left in the ground throughout the winter, provided slugs are

WATERING METHODS

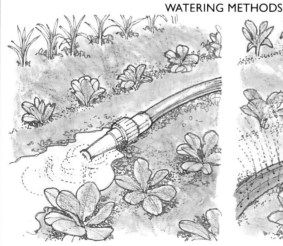

Water seedlings and young transplants with a hosepipe. Make sure you turn the flow down to a steady trickle. Only when the plants are sturdier should you use automatic watering.

A perforated flat hose, the upper surface of which has thousands of minute holes, gives a fine upward spray of water. Lay it along the ground between rows of vegetables.

A basket of home-grown produce, picked when the vegetables are at the peak of perfection.

Radishes are best picked when they are still quite small. Left in the soil for too long they may become woody and even hollow.

not a problem. Parsnips are said to improve in flavour if left in the ground until after a frost. In mild parts of the country, celeriac can stay in the ground – hard northern winters, however, tend to be a little too severe.

Although celery probably improves with age fairly consistently, it is not all that hardy. The trench varieties which have the benefit of added protection from earthing-up, can be left in the ground, however.

Below: Gently lift out leeks with a fork, when they are still fairly young. The flavour deteriorates as they grow larger.

A–Z OF VEGETABLES

Where possible, the information on each vegetable crop has been standardized under a sequence of headings to make it easier to find what you want to know. However, as with every aspect of gardening, there are a hundred ways of doing every job, all perfectly satisfactory in their own right, so do not be afraid to experiment or feel bound to follow all the recommendations here.

When planning and cultivating a vegetable garden the rule is to be flexible. Remember that it is quite difficult to do anything drastically wrong – in fact, it is far more likely that you will develop new methods which are ideally suited to your own location and growing conditions.

Before launching into the A–Z here are a few general remarks on the information included under some of the headings in this chapter.

VARIETIES
Generally each crop has a large number of varieties and they have so many pros and cons that choosing is difficult even for the expert. Only the most popular and reliable ones, in order of preference, have been included here.

GROWING TIME
Because local and seasonal variations can be important factors, the figures given can only be an average indication of the length of time a particular crop will take up space, and how long you will have to wait before you can eat it. The figures will help you to determine whether the crop concerned is worth trying.

SOWING AND PLANTING
Sowing dates cannot be hard and fast because there may be snow or frost on the day you intend, for example, to prepare the parsnip bed. During a cold late spring, it may also pay to delay sowing by a week or two. Indoor sowing, of course, will not be affected by the weather. Where sowing under glass is recommended, this can also

Globe artichokes are harvested in June and July. Pick when they are still tightly wrapped, using a pair of secateurs and leave some of the stem attached.

be taken to mean windowsill sowing.

Slightly closer or wider spacing may be more convenient or practical in some circumstances. Pot sizes are given where applicable, but don't worry if the right-sized one is not to hand; make do with the next size.

Broad dates are given for crops which require transplanting or planting out rather than being sown *in situ*. Useful tips, such as whether firm planting or extra fertilizer is advisable at planting time, are also given.

Often, the average width of a mature plant gives an indication of the space the whole crop will take up in the plot. In recent years, however, growing schemes other than the normal row system have

become popular, so the number of plants accommodated in 1 sq m (1 sq yd) of soil has been given.

POSSIBLE PROBLEMS
These include pests, diseases, nutritional disorders and other hazards peculiar to the vegetable concerned. Tips are given on how to deal with them.

ARTICHOKE, GLOBE
A thistle-like perennial of the daisy family, grown for its edible petals and the flower heart or 'fond' under the hairy seed 'choke'. Its delicate flavour is highly thought of by gourmets, but it is a large plant, up to 1·5 m (5 ft) tall, and takes up a lot of space

for a comparatively small yield over a relatively short season. Only grow it if you are passionate about the vegetable or you own a large plot of land.

Soil Medium to light, rich soil with good drainage is best, but any fertile soil will produce some results. Any amount of well rotted manure, compost or peat incorporated into the soil will be appreciated by the plants.

Planting In spring – late March or April – plant strong rooted offsets (basal shoots growing from a parent plant) at least 25 cm (10 in) high, 90 cm (3 ft) apart in the row and between rows. Ensure the rooted base is planted firmly to just above the old soil line on the stem, and at least 5 cm (2 in) deep. Water in well and keep watered until new growth has begun.

Allow one plant per sq m (sq yd).

Cultivation In dry weather water copiously. Mulch when established and every spring thereafter.

Hoe around young plants regularly. Like all permanent residents of a plot, artichokes attract perennial weeds – bindweed and couch grass can be carefully treated with glyphosate gel and alloxydim sodium, respectively.

Feed regularly: top dress in spring each year and liquid feed with a concentrated soluble food regularly in summer.

Protect the crowns from frost in the winter. Cover with their own leaves as they die down, and bracken, straw or peat.

Possible problems Almost trouble-free. Blackfly and slugs may require treatment.

Growing time Planting to cropping, 18–24 months.

Harvesting Cut off all flower buds as soon as they form in the first year. Cut for eating from the second year; remove the large centre bud first and progress to the side buds as they develop. Pick when the bud is fat and green but before the petals begin to open. Cutting may last for three months from late June in some years, but normally finishes a little earlier.

Special points Beautiful, tall, silvery foliaged plants that would grace any herbaceous border if the space is not available in the vegetable plot. Every spring, remove and plant rooted suckers from established plants, which are relatively short-lived, to obtain a succession.

Varieties 'Biarritz': the largest amount of edible flesh and best flavour, but is not reliably hardy except in the south. 'Vert de Laon': a good second choice.

ARTICHOKE, JERUSALEM

A tall tuberous-rooted perennial of the daisy family, more closely related to sunflowers than to thistles. It reaches 2·4 m (8 ft) or more, and its knobbly root tubers have a flavour similar to the flowers of the globe artichoke. The quantity of tubers, their nutritional value and ease of cultivation make this crop more worth growing than the globe artichoke.

Soil Any soil will do with the exception, perhaps, of acid sands and peats. Manure from the previous crop is ideal – the number of tubers is less and slug damage worse if fresh manure is used.

Planting Plant small to medium tubers in February or March, 45 cm (18 in) apart and 15 cm (6 in) deep, with the pointed nose of the tuber upwards. One row, used as a screen or windbreak, will probably be enough, but if not, space other rows 90 cm (3 ft) apart. Unlike almost any other vegetables bought at supermarkets for eating, its tubers can be used for planting. Named varieties, of course, should be better.

Allow three plants per sq m (sq yd).

Cultivation Extra watering is unlikely to be necessary, although drought may reduce the number and size of the crop.

Ridge the soil around the stem bases as

Jerusalem artichokes reach up to 2·4 m (8 ft) tall so they need some form of support. Drive a stake into the ground at the end of the rows and then run strong cord between the stakes.

Asparagus spears should be cut when they are about 10 cm (4 in) above the ground. Make your cut 7·5 cm (3 in) below the soil surface.

ASPARAGUS

An unlikely member of the lily family, grown for its new leaf stem shoots or spears which are cut as they appear through the ground in the spring. A sought-after gourmet delicacy, but can only be considered if you have a large garden because it occupies a lot of land for a long time.

Soil Completely weed-free and well drained soil is more important than fertility. Digging and preparing the trench the previous autumn, incorporating a good dressing of organic manure in the bottom spit is ideal, but the standard soil preparation for a vegetable plot will produce a perfectly satisfactory crop.

Sowing and planting 'Connover's Colossal' can be raised from seed, but it will be three years from sowing to the first cut. Sow in April in a standard seed bed, 13 mm ($\frac{1}{2}$ in) deep; thin seedlings to 15 cm (6 in) apart and grow on until the following spring.

In April, plant the one-year 'crowns' 30–45 cm (12–18 in) apart in a prepared trench 30 cm (12 in) wide and 20 cm (8 in) deep, with the roots spread evenly over a central mound or ridge. Cover the crowns with about 5 cm (2 in) of soil and gradually fill the remainder of the trench as the plants grow, until it is level with the surrounding soil.

Allow six to nine asparagus plants per sq m (sq yd).

Cultivation Humus in the soil and an annual mulch of manure in autumn will retain water in all but the driest weather, when the plants must be well watered.

Weed the bed regularly by hand and use a selective weedkiller. Any garden weedkiller containing '2,4-D' will kill weeds without harming asparagus, although it always pays to follow the instructions carefully. However, do not spray the plants deliberately.

Around established beds, posts and wires should be used to support the floppy ferny growth of the mature plants.

Possible problems Rarely, violet root rot can virtually destroy a whole asparagus bed; plants wilt and die and the roots

they grow. They will root into this and give themselves valuable extra support for later in the year when they are top heavy and offer a great deal of wind resistance. Knock in a robust stake at each end of the row, and run strong rope each side of the row about halfway up the plants to help stabilize them.

Possible problems A remarkably trouble-free crop, other than from slugs; the sweet, starch-free tubers seem to attract them from miles around. Plant with slug pellets or slug tape and water with a liquid slug killer, based on metaldehyde or the less noxious copper sulphate.

Growing time From planting to digging 10–12 months.

Harvesting The odd plant can be dug up for a summer meal of small tubers, but

the majority do not reach maximum size until about October, or even later in northern districts. The tubers are hardy and can be left in the ground until wanted. Cut down the stems to about 30 cm (12 in) to lower wind resistance. Slugs may be a problem on tubers left in the soil, so some can be lifted, packed in boxes of moist sand or peat and stored in a cold, dry and frost-free place.

Special points Rotation of such large plants may pose a problem and it is fortunate that they do not seem to deteriorate appreciably when grown in the same soil for several years.

Varieties There is nothing to choose between the few that are available but 'Fuseau' has the edge because its tuber is a little smoother skinned than that of the other varieties.

Pick asparagus peas when they are still small or they will become stringy. The pods are eaten whole and have a flavour reminiscent of asparagus, hence the name.

turn mouldy and purple. There is no cure – make a new bed in another part of the garden and do not use the affected area for at least three years.

The little black and orange asparagus beetle and its grub may severely damage leaves and stems which are stripped. Spray with permethrin, derris or a special insecticidal liquid soft soap in the evening.

Growing time From planting to first cropping, 24 months.

Harvesting New plants are left to settle in and enlarge their crowns for two whole seasons after planting. It is only in their third season, 24 months or so after planting, that a few spears can be cut from each plant. From this time onwards all the spears can be cut when they are 10 cm (4 in) above ground. Cut the spears about 7·5 cm (3 in) below ground with a sharp knife. Cutting can continue until about mid June when the plants must be allowed to grow and build up crowns for the next year's crop.

Special points Once planted, an asparagus bed will not crop until its third year, but it could then go on cropping for 20 years. So thorough preparation, additional spring mulching and top dressing, and liquid feeding in summer after cutting has finished, will pay dividends.

Varieties 'Connover's Colossal': a safe, reliable, heavy cropper if conditions are right. 'Lucullus': seems set to take over as the favourite; it has all the advantages of the former variety and it is an all-male variety, the significance of this being that there will be no self-sown seedlings to adulterate the crop or berrying females of reduced vigour.

ASPARAGUS PEA

This legume is not a true pea, but a type of annual vetch, grown for its curiously shaped pods, which are eaten whole like a mangetout pea. The pods have a slight flavour of asparagus, so it can best be described as a novelty vegetable.

Soil As for the garden pea (see page 68).

Sowing and planting Rows, 38 cm (15 in) apart. Sow seed 7·5 cm (3 in) apart, 5 cm (2 in) deep. Thin seedlings to 30 cm (12 in) apart. Under glass: in early April in pots for planting out in early June (it is not frost hardy). Outdoors: during May. The indoor sowings should be planted out when about 2·5 cm (1 in) high.

Cultivation Similar to ordinary garden peas in its requirements and it, too, needs pea sticks for support.

Possible problems It tends to crop far less than peas but, by way of compensation, has fewer ailments.

Growing time 70 days.

Harvesting Pick frequently as soon as the pods are 2·5 cm (1 in) long, before they become stringy from June to August.

Varieties Only the species, *Tetragonolobus purpureus*, is available.

AUBERGINE

Widely known as the egg plant, this is an annual member of the tomato family. Because of its tenderness, it can only be grown in a sunny sheltered site in mild gardens or in a greenhouse. Aubergines make small bushes up to 75 cm (30 in) high; their fruits are of a less distinct flavour than the tomato. Most varieties are black-skinned but you can also grow white-skinned ones.

Soil Like the tomato, the aubergine is a heavy feeder and adequate fertilizer is more important than rich soil, although it is best to have good drainage and, in the greenhouse, to use sterile seed and potting composts. Growing bags are excellent for aubergines.

Sowing and planting In a temperature of at least 18·5°C (65°F), sow two seeds in a peat pot of soilless compost, in February for a greenhouse crop and in March for an outdoor crop. Take out the weaker seedling when the first true leaves are visible and grow on until they have six to eight leaves before planting, complete with pot, in April in the greenhouse and May under cloches. Harden off outdoor plants, and plant 60 cm (2 ft) apart in rows. Water in well.

Cultivation When the plants reach 30 cm (12 in) high pinch out the growing tips to make them produce more fruiting side shoots. Put in canes for support and, as the plants grow, tie the stems to the canes with string.

Possible problems Aubergines are not prey to most of the troubles of tomatoes, but they can be badly affected by red spider mite, whitefly and aphids, all of which are very persistent. Control these pests with a spray programme using a plant extract or refined pure soap insecticide.

Feed regularly, preferably at every watering once the first fruit has begun to swell. Use a high-potash, soluble tomato feed which, usefully, contains extra magnesium and calcium.

Growing time 140 days.

Harvesting Picking extends over about two-and-a-half months between July and October, although outdoors this could end by September. Choose firm, ripe fruit 10–15 cm (4–6 in), and pick while still glossy. Older fruit can be tough and tart. Cut the fruit stems to avoid damaging the plant with secateurs rather than tearing them off.

Special points Keeping the air humid, but buoyant, and misting over the plants with clean soft water will encourage the fruit to set, as well as discouraging red spider mite.

Varieties 'Black Enorma': produces the largest aubergines of all. 'Black Prince': an F1 hybrid; heavier cropper than the reliable old favourite 'Long Purple'. 'Easter Egg': a white-skinned egg-shaped novelty with a milder flavour than most.

Aubergines will only thrive and produce ripe fruit outdoors in the mildest parts of the country. They must be grown in a warm, sunny and sheltered corner.

Allow 100–120 days between sowing and harvesting broad beans. After the crop has been harvested, dig the plants into the ground as a green manure.

BEAN, BROAD

The hardiest of the beans; standard types are up to 1 m (3 ft) high, dwarf types 30–45 cm (12–18 in). Spring sown only; autumn sowing is only considered worthwhile by experienced growers, except possibly in mild areas.

Soil Any good soil, preferably free-draining and not too acid; apply manure or compost in autumn or winter and fertilizer a week before sowing or planting out.

Sowing and planting Double rows, 20 cm (8 in) apart and 60 cm (2 ft) between each pair of rows. Seeds 20 cm (8 in) apart and 5 cm (2 in) deep. Outdoors: February to May, except in the south where October to December is possible. Under cloches, in a cold frame or cold greenhouse, January to March. Plants from seed sown indoors can be hardened off and planted out from March onwards.
Allow five plants per sq m (sq yd).

Cultivation In an average year watering should not be necessary until the pods begin to swell, then water thoroughly in dry weather.
Young plants are easily swamped by weeds; frequent hoeing is probably the easiest way of keeping these down. Staking large plants may be necessary, especially in windy weather – a cane at each corner of the growing area with string encircling the crop is an alternative and wise precaution. Pinch out the top shoots of each plant when the first flowers have set pods – this gives an earlier crop and deters blackfly which are attracted to the softer green growth.

Possible problems Blackfly on young shoots are best picked off. Chocolate spot is a fungus disease that looks just as it sounds; feed well with a high potash fertilizer to prevent it.

Growing time 100–120 days.

Harvesting June to September; pick as often as possible; small, young beans are more tender and tastier, so pick when no more than 7·5 cm (3 in) long to encourage the maximum crop. Mature beans for winter use should be picked when the pods begin to shrink (but before they actually shrivel) and the shape of the seeds can be clearly seen.

Special points Dig in the whole plant after picking is finished as a green manure, or cut off the stems and leave the roots to decay and return the nitrogen fertilizer from their root nodules to the soil.

Varieties 'Aquadulce Claudia': a large white-beaned long pod variety, very hardy and reliable cropper. 'Masterpiece': early cropping, green-beaned long pod variety; strong flavour, suitable for freezing. 'The Sutton': dwarf, white-beaned, short podded variety; good for early sowing and cropping under cloches.

BEAN, KIDNEY (FRENCH)

These are frost tender. They have rounder but smaller pods than runner beans. Most types produce small bushy plants up to 45 cm (18 in) high. One or two climbing varieties reach up to 1·5 m (5 ft). Well worth growing.

Soil They dislike acid soil and prefer it not too heavy. Use manure or compost the previous autumn and lime, if acid, three or four weeks before sowing.

Sowing and planting Rows 45 cm (18 in) apart. Seeds 10 cm (4 in) apart, 5 cm (2 in) deep. Under glass: March to April. Outdoors: May to July, two or three successional sowings, about three weeks apart, will prolong cropping.
Although usually sown *in situ*, a few seeds sown in pots or boxes will provide replacements for the inevitable losses in early sowings.
Allow nine plants per sq m (sq yd).

Cultivation Soak thoroughly in dry weather when flowering or picking.
Weeds may swamp young plants; hoe carefully, for they are very easily chopped off at ground level. Pea sticks prevent floppy plants falling over.

Possible problems Blackfly and, especially on the dwarf varieties, slugs may damage the pods.

Growing time 60–90 days.

Harvesting Late June to early November if early sowings and late crops are protected under cloches. Pick several times a week to keep the young beans coming. Small pods that snap easily and which have no sign of the beans showing through the skin are the tastiest and least stringy. Leaving pods on the plant until yellowing, before final drying and shelling indoors, will provide a supply of haricot beans for winter use.

Special points Liquid feeding is especially beneficial and after the main picking will encourage a second, although smaller, flush of pods.

Varieties 'Masterpiece': an early, but heavy cropper. 'Canadian Wonder': heavy crop, good flavour but often difficult to find. 'Remus': crisp and sweet, beans held above leaves for convenience and protection from mud splashes. 'Blue Lake': heavy cropping climber. 'Blue Coco': purple-podded climber, very good flavour, attractive plants.

BEAN, RUNNER

A perennial, usually grown as an annual. The most vigorous bean, climbing up to 3·7 m (12 ft) and making a useful screen as well as a most acceptable vegetable. It makes an attractive plant grown up walls or even an arch.

Soil Rich, light, well drained, non-acid soil produces the best crops. Dig a traditional bean trench in autumn, with a good deep layer of well rotted manure or compost at the bottom before refilling. Leave for the winter and earth over with fresh soil from the sides; lime only if soil is very acid and top dress with fertilizer a week or two before sowing or planting out.

Sowing and planting Rows 45 cm (18 in) apart. Sow 20 cm (8 in) apart, 5 cm (2 in) deep. Under glass: mid March to late April. Outdoors: mid May to July.
Plant seedlings raised under glass in

late May to early June. Outside, take care to harden seedlings off gradually or protect with cloches for the first week or so.
Allow nine plants per sq m (sq yd).

Cultivation Water regularly and very thoroughly in dry weather. Mulching is useful with such thirsty plants to discourage evaporation from the soil.
Hoe regularly and watch for bindweed hiding in the twining bean stems. Liquid feeding is appreciated and foliar feeding is very effective. Pinch out the shoot tips at the tops of the supports.

Possible problems Large colonies of blackfly can stunt growth and cause distorted pods. Look out for them in summer.

Growing time 90 days.

Harvesting Mid July to late October or early November, depending on season and locality. It is important to keep picking young beans to prevent the plants ceasing production. Such high yields and cropping rates mean that, at some point, there is bound to be a surfeit; so a deep freeze is a priceless asset.

Special points Watering with lime water, a handful of garden lime in a 9 litre (2 gallon) watering can, may be effective in poor set years. Spraying with water or sugar solution does not improve 'set'. Pinching out the growing points as soon as the seedling stems begin to twine will

Pick the runner beans when the pods reach 15–20 cm (6–8 in) long. This will encourage the plants to continue producing a healthy crop for at least two months.

VEGETABLE GARDENING

With their scarlet flowers and rambling habit, runner beans make attractive plants for training up arches and arbours. This releases ground in the vegetable patch for growing other crops.

produce shorter plants and earlier, but smaller, crops.

Varieties 'Achievement', 'Enorma' and 'Streamline': all for sheer quantity. 'Kelvedon Marvel' and 'Kelvedon Wonder': shorter, earlier and substantial croppers. 'Red Knight': a good freezer, with excellent flavour and stringless.

BEETROOT

A biennial root crop with more or less round or cylindrical roots projecting above soil level. Dark red varieties have always been preferred in this country; there are white and golden types as well. Grown for salads and for winter storage.

Soil Deep, light or sandy soils produce the best beetroot. Deep digging will make most soils suitable, but only use land that has not been freshly manured for at least a year; fresh manure or compost produces 'fanging' or forked roots. On very light, poor soils you will find an extra dressing of a soluble tomato food or any of the high-potash fertilizers will increase the results dramatically.

Sowing and planting Rows 30 cm (12 in) apart. Sow seeds 10 cm (4 in) apart, 2·5 cm (1 in) deep. Seeds appear to be relatively large but in reality are small capsules containing more than one seed. Sow two capsules at each position and pull out all but the strongest seedling when about 2·5 cm (1 in) high.

Under glass (cloches): sow seeds from late February. Outdoors: sow seeds from early April to July.

Beetroots, like other root crops, tend to produce split or forked roots if transplanted, but this does not happen if seed is sown in peat pots and these are planted out without disturbing the young roots from late April.

Allow 35 plants per sq m (sq yd).

Cultivation Lack of water causes toughness while excess water can cause the roots to split; evenly moist soil is the answer and regular moderate watering the safeguard.

With such a relatively low growing crop, weeding is vital. Weedkillers can be most useful if applied correctly and carefully – it is easy to damage seedlings and young, swelling roots by carelessly wielding the hoe.

Possible problems Susceptible to trace element deficiencies. Lack of boron causes dark, soft areas on the skin and heart rot. Shortage of manganese shows as curled, yellow leaves. Both will be prevented by using plenty of manure in previous years (see crop rotation, pages 25 to 28). Foliar feeding with a soluble plant food may help reduce the symptoms, which are aggravated by liming the soil.

Growing time 90–120 days.

For the best beetroot, grow on a light or sandy soil which has been dug deeply, but not manured for at least one year.

BRASSICAS

Brassicas are members of the cabbage family, a group that includes broccoli, Brussels sprouts, cabbage, cauliflower, calabrese and kale – all leaf crops – as well as kohl rabi (or turnip-rooted cabbage), swede and turnip.

Because of their close relationship they like the same soils and cultural conditions. In order to save repetition, their common requirements are given here, while the special needs of a particular crop are reserved for their individual entries.

Soil Although brassicas have a reputation for liking lime, they do not thrive in very limy or chalky soil. In fact, they prefer slightly acid conditions and only very acid soils will need liming (see page 12). They require a deep, fertile soil – one of the commonest reasons for failure is a lack of organic manure and fertilizer. A good dressing of manure, no later than the previous autumn, will pay dividends, but this must be dug in long enough before planting to allow the soil to settle again thoroughly; the manuring for the previous year's crop may be sufficient if it was heavy enough. Strangely, for such strong growing, deep rooted vegetables, loosening the soil is not advisable since they must have firm foundations to grow into. Just light hoeing and raking to remove surface weeds is recommended.

Planting The timing of planting out varies with the type and variety concerned, but all should be planted very firmly. Try to keep a good root system with plenty of soil attached, and make the planting holes with a dibber and not a trowel. Make the hole about 10 cm (4 in) deep and 'puddle-in' the plants by pouring water into the hole before covering the roots. Then make another hole alongside the first and lever the dibber towards the plant to compress the soil around its roots. Tread the soil firmly around each plant and fill the hollow you make with water. Keep the

Newly planted 'Hispi', a variety of spring cabbage grown for its delicious flavour. Medium-sized, compact and quick maturing, this is an excellent choice for a small plot.

Protect your brassicas from the ravages of pigeons by stretching nylon netting over the plants, making sure they are completely covered. Pigeons can destroy an entire crop by eating the soft parts of the leaves.

transplants watered and shaded for the next two or three weeks.

Cultivation Never let brassicas go short of water. Unless the weather is constantly wet, keep the soil deeply and evenly moist, especially for seedlings and new transplants. Up to 20 litres per sq m (4 gallons per sq yd) will not be excessive for a strongly growing established crop.

Extra top dressing with fertilizer will be needed in mid summer or, alternatively, regular liquid feeding will produce more succulent plants, particularly in drier years. The taller brassicas – Brussels sprouts and broccoli – may need staking in case there are winter gales. Earthing-up the stems and, firming the soil also helps.

Possible problems Brassicas can be prey to a wide range of pests and diseases, but most are quickly recognized and easily dealt with by the methods outlined in the chapter on Pests and Diseases. Of these, pigeons, slugs and caterpillars are the most common; others are comparatively rare. There are three problems that require special attention.

Club root: this fungus disease, also known as 'finger and toe' disease, causes club-like swollen roots and dramatically reduces the crop yield. The disease cannot be effectively removed from the soil, where it lies dormant for many years, so brassicas should be grown on the patch as infrequently as possible.

Liming discourages it and in recent years this treatment has been preferred to the application of mercurous chloride, benomyl or thiophanate-methyl club root dips. The latter can be used to puddle-in the transplants by making a thin watery paste and dipping the roots in it before planting them out. Perhaps the most satisfactory way of overcoming the problem is to grow your own plants from seeds sown in sterile seed compost, potting on into 12·5 cm (5 in) pots of sterile potting compost and planting out with their undisturbed root ball.

Cabbage root fly: grubs from eggs laid in the soil bore into the stem at ground level and cause the plant to wilt easily and perhaps die. Raising seedlings and potting them on in sterile compost allows bromophos or diazinon to be incorporated with the compost at the same time.

Cabbage mealy aphid: this aphid is particularly difficult to deal with as it always hides under the leaves and its mealy, waxy coating prevents sprays from wetting it thoroughly, with the result that insecticides are ineffective. The new refined and safer soap sprays, with their combined insecticidal and wetting properties, are better.

Red cabbages are sown outdoors in spring and harvested in the autumn. If you cut them in late autumn they can be stored over the winter.

Sow winter cabbage outdoors in May for cutting from November onwards. Cook them immediately after harvesting.

Broccoli is not the easiest of brassicas to grow but your efforts will be rewarded with a delicious crop. It is harvested by cutting a few shoots from each plant at a time. You should expect another picking six to eight weeks later.

Harvesting May to October with those to be stored for winter mainly pulled in July to September. Thin out small roots, up to 4 cm (1½ in) in diameter, by pulling every other plant – use these for cooking. Always pull before the roots become large and woody, showing white rings inside. Always twist off the foliage to discourage bleeding. Store mature crops pulled in September and October in boxes of peat. Lift carefully and do not break or bruise the skins or rot will set in during storage.

Special points Use netting to protect seedlings from birds. Single seeded varieties like 'Monopoly' and pelleted seeds are available which, sown singly, do away with the need to thin or 'single' plants.

Varieties 'Boltardy': a bolt resistant type as its name suggests – i.e. it does not easily run to seed before producing a good root. 'Avonearly': an equally popular red beetroot. 'Burpee's Golden' and 'Snowhite': yellow and white varieties respectively, the former being particularly interesting because it does not bleed.

BROCCOLI

A hardy flowering brassica, with flower spikes similar to small cauliflowers, but with a more delicate flavour. It makes a delectable vegetable, but does take up a great deal of space and time. Calabrese, a half-hardy continental type, is dealt with separately (see page 51). Consult brassicas (pages 46 to 47) for cultivation.

Soil Good drainage is preferred and is more essential than for some brassicas.

Sowing and planting Rows 15 cm (6 in) apart. Seeds 13 mm (½ in) deep and no less then 13 mm (½ in) apart. Remove the weakest seedlings to leave about 7·5 cm (3 in) between plants at transplanting time. Sow in mid April and May. If club root is a problem sow in sterile compost in a cold frame. Lift seedlings carefully and plant firmly from early June to early August.
Allow two plants per sq m (sq yd).

Possible problems To prevent wind rock, earth up; refirm by treading and re-stake if necessary.

Growing time 300 days.

Harvesting Early varieties are usually ready for cutting between February and March, late ones in late March to mid May. Cut frequently, while in tight bud, taking a few shoots at a time and cutting the central spike first. Plants will then re-crop over six to eight weeks. A good freezer vegetable – blanch for three minutes after soaking in salt water for fifteen minutes.

Special points These are not the easiest brassica to grow.

Varieties 'Early' and 'Late Purple Sprouting': very hardy and useful for winter vegetables in cold areas. 'White Sprouting': also has early and late varieties, but tastes more like a cauli-flower, and may be a little less hardy in severe winters.

BRUSSELS SPROUTS

The tallest brassica and one of the hardiest. Larger varieties grow 1·2 m (4 ft) tall. All reliable winter croppers. Takes up a lot of time and space, but such a reliable and popular winter vegetable is indispensable. (See brassicas, pages 46 to 47 for cultivation details.)

Soil Brussels sprouts need the firmest soil of all brassicas. Leave the soil for several months before planting; do not dig, and firm thoroughly by treading around young plants, repeating this frequently as they establish.

Sowing and planting Rows 15 cm (6 in) apart. Seeds 13 mm (½ in) deep and no less than 13 mm (½ in) apart. Under glass: late February to early March. Outdoors: mid March to mid April. Remove the weakest seedlings to leave about 7·5 cm (3 in) between plants at transplanting time. Lift plants carefully with as little damage to roots as possible and replant very firmly between late April (indoor sown) and late June (outdoor sown).
Allow two to four plants per sq m (sq yd).

Possible problems Buttons 'blown' or opening, usually caused by poor infertile soil, loose planting or insufficient water. Wind rock can be severe; earth-up, refirm by stamping in, and stake the plants if it is necessary.

Growing time 200–250 days, depending on variety.

Harvesting Picking on individual

plants can be over two or three months, especially with the selected varieties, and runs from mid to later September through to about April in an average year. Pick progressively from the bottom up, a few sprouts at a time. F1 varieties tend to have even buttons so pick these when they appear at their best. Delaying the start of picking until after the first frost is claimed to improve the flavour.

Cabbages do take up a large amount of space, so they are best grown only in fairly extensive plots.

'Widgeon' is an F1 hybrid Brussels sprout.

Special points Do not skimp on the fertilizer base dressing and give extra liquid top dressing in the summer, but do not give any nitrogen fertilizer after August as this may produce a slightly bitter flavour.

Varieties 'Peer Gynt' and 'Citadel': early and main season F1 hybrids produc-ing well flavoured, uniform buttons. 'Roodnerf-Seven Hills' with long lasting tight sprouts, 'Bedford Fillbasket' with large sprouts and 'Rubine', red sprout of unique flavour, are not F1 hybrids so need picking carefully as they reach their peak.

CABBAGE

A hardy, single-headed brassica which includes some of the fastest and longest growing green vegetables. Four types make cabbage the longest cropping vege-table by far. There should not be a month when they are not available – they may be scarcer in June or July, but with a little practice these months can easily be covered, too. The long cutting season and ease of cultivation make cabbages desir-able vegetables, although they do take up a large amount of space and time con-sidering that most provide only one picking, and the spring types use valuable summer vegetable space.

Soil Not quite so dependent on firm soil as other brassicas.

Sowing and planting Rows 15 cm (6 in) apart. Seeds, 13 mm ($\frac{1}{2}$ in) deep, not less than 13 mm ($\frac{1}{2}$ in) apart. Remove the

PICKING BRUSSELS SPROUTS

1. As the plants grow, pick off any yellow leaves or loose-leaved sprouts from the bottom of the stem. This will create better air circulation.

2. When the sprouts are ready to harvest – they should be small and compact – pick from the base upwards. There is an old saying, that they taste better after a slight frost.

weakest seedlings to leave about 7·5 mm (3 in) between the plants at transplanting time. Sow spring cabbage outdoors, July in cold or northern areas, August in warm southern areas. Summer cabbages: under glass, February and March; outdoors, March to early May. Winter cabbages: outdoors April and May. Savoy cabbages: outdoors, April and May.

Allow seedlings to establish well with six or more leaves before transplanting. Plant spring cabbages early, 12 cm (5 in) apart to give greens from the thinnings. The others, 30–45 cm (12–18 in) apart depending on type and variety. Follow any instructions on the seed packets.

Allow for up to five plants per sq m (sq yd) for winter, summer and Savoy types and ten to eleven for spring types.

Cultivation Keep well watered as heads reach maturity, and liquid feed with high-potash fertilizer. (See brassicas, pages 46 to 47, for cultivation.)

Possible problems Some varieties are prone to splitting in cold weather.

Growing time Summer varieties: 120–200 days; winter and Savoy varieties: 150–240 days; spring varieties: 240 days.

Harvesting Spring types, April to August; summer types, July to November; winter types, October to March. Spring cabbage planted extra thickly can be cut as spring greens from March onwards until the remaining plants are 30–45 cm (12–18 in) apart. Store cut winter cabbages in straw after trimming off outer leaves and roots. Winter variety 'Jupiter' will store hanging up by its roots. Early cabbages can be induced to produce

CABBAGE PROTECTION
Brassica collars can be put around the stems of cabbages, after transplanting to prevent cabbage root fly (a common brassica pest) damaging the root systems.

several more smaller heads if a cross cut is made in the flat surface of the remaining plant stem.

Cabbages are not the best brassicas to freeze, but very firm heads which are blanched for one minute are reasonably satisfactory.

Varieties Spring cabbages: 'Spring Hero': a very solid medium to heavy weight F1 round-headed variety; 'Durham Early': a pointed-head type which produces darker spring greens. Summer cabbages: 'Hispi' and 'Spitfire' are both fast growing pointed-head F 1 varieties. 'Hispi' is a little earlier and 'Golden Acre', a solid round-head, cuts about the same time. Red cabbages: not great favourites, but just as tasty and even more attractive raw in salads, a late summer type – a small but reliable, solid plant. Winter cabbages: the new 'Celtic' F1 is the best variety, split-free even in the hardest weather; the F1 'Jupiter' keeps well when stored whole in a shed or outhouse. Savoy cabbages are crinkle-leaved winter cabbages: 'Savoy King' is an F1 which has all the best features of this type – a gentler, less peppery taste, extreme hardiness and less demanding of good soil and fertilizer, which makes it an easy variety to grow.

Calabrese is not fully hardy, so it is grown outdoors in summer for picking before the arrival of winter.

CALABRESE

A green, fast growing Italian version of our purple and white sprouting broccoli. Much smaller than either of these, it is usually under 60 cm (2 ft) high and not fully hardy in winter. Its short growing period, smaller size and delicate flavour make this a good vegetable to grow if you have space during summer, but it can be temperamental, like its brassica relative the cauliflower.

Soil Water conservation, especially in light soils, must be improved with adequate organic manure.

Sowing and planting Sowings *in situ:* rows, 30 cm (12 in) apart. Seeds 13 mm ($\frac{1}{2}$ in) deep, 15 cm (6 in) apart. Sow three seeds per position and pull out the two weakest when the first true leaves are formed. First sowings, April to May; successional sowings, two or three in June and July. For transplanting, sow into 7·5 cm (3 in) pots of sterile loam-based seed compost. Sow three seeds per pot and thin to leave the strongest seedling in each pot.

Almost alone amongst the brassicas, calabrese objects strongly to the upheaval caused by transplanting. For earlier crops and protection from club root or cabbage root fly, use the pot sowing method to plant out without disturbing the roots unnecessarily.

Allow 20 plants per sq m (sq yd).

Cultivation Keeping the soil evenly moist at all times is as important for calabrese as it is for the other flowering brassicas.

Possible problems Lack of water, especially at critical periods such as in the seed bed or when the flower spikes are forming, will cause bolting and produce small, inferior heads. Caterpillars can hide more easily in the open heads; soak the calabrese in salt water before cooking if this pest is suspected.

Growing time 90–150 days.

Harvesting The picking of calabrese usually starts about July but can be as early as June if pot grown transplants are used instead.

Capsicums (sweet peppers) can be grown outdoors in mild parts of the country, but raise the seeds under glass first. Outdoor plants usually reach only 60 cm (2 ft) high.

Cut the central spike first – this is often quite large, resembling a small green cauliflower. The side shoots on each plant will then develop over the next two or three weeks. Cut only a few spikes at a time when the flower buds are lightly closed.

CAPSICUM

The sweet pepper is an annual member of the tomato family, but it has a more distinct flavour and crisper texture than either the tomato or the aubergine. A valuable greenhouse crop, it is also reliable outdoors in most years. Its light, sweet peppery taste and crisp, crunchy texture, lends itself perfectly to salads.

Site and soil Sun and shelter are necessary and the soil should be fertile, well-drained and with a general fertilizer added before planting.

Sowing and planting Treat capsicum seeds in exactly the same way as when sowing and planting aubergines (see pages 40 to 41), except that you should plant out the seedlings with 45 cm (18 in) gaps between plants and rows.

Cultivation The growing requirements are virtually identical to that of aubergines, with two important exceptions. First, the plants must not have a check to growth and need frequent repotting up to planting out size. Second, do not pinch out capsicums; they are naturally bushy plants.

Possible problems Capsicums have a tendency, like tomatoes, to blossom-end rot if they suffer from lack of water or calcium when the fruits are swelling. This condition appears up to two weeks after the shortage that caused it.

Growing time 120 days.

Harvesting Again the same as aubergines, between July and October, with the likelihood that picking will finish earlier outdoors. Cut the fruits off, starting when the first ones are fully grown but still green, to induce further flowering. Like tomatoes, sweet peppers will ripen off the plant – more quickly in a warm place than a cold one.

Varieties 'Canape': an F1 hybrid, a good variety for greenhouse and outdoor growing. 'Ace': possibly even more tolerant of cold summers.

CARROTS

The carrot is a biennial (it would flower in its second year), but it is harvested in the same year as sowing. An essential crop, the early, short types are considered to have the edge over the later, longer rooted varieties.

Soil Deep, light, and preferably sandy soil is best for carrots. Light but shallow soils may grow a good crop of 'Kundulus' or another short- or ball-rooted variety. Root crops always come at the end of the rotation cycle when there is the least organic manure in the soil.

Sowing and planting Rows 15 cm (6 in) apart. Sow seeds 13 mm ($\frac{1}{2}$ in) deep, very thinly along the drill. Under glass (cloches): short-rooted in late February to early March. Outdoors: short-rooted in March to July; successively every two or three weeks for a constant supply of fresh carrots. Intermediate- and long-rooted in April to June for later, maincrop carrots.

Root crops, including carrots, do not generally stand transplanting because the inevitable damage to the single tap root causes distorted growth and often double roots. They can, however, be raised in peat pots and planted out, pot and all; this will produce show quality carrots. In the garden, the seedlings are grown *in situ* and thinned progressively (the thinnings can be eaten) until the remaining plants are about 3·5 cm (1$\frac{1}{2}$ in) apart.

Allow 80 intermediate- and long-rooted varieties and 144 short-rooted varieties per sq m (sq yd).

Maincrop carrots are lifted between August and October. Loosen the ground with a fork first and then clean off the soil.

The maggots of carrot fly tunnel into the roots and may cause them to rot. They are more of a problem on dry soils.

Cultivation Keep the soil moist by watering in dry periods, otherwise sudden heavy rainfall may cause root splitting.

Annual weeds are unlikely to be a problem in the row but keep an eye open for the odd perennial weed creeping in; between the rows, hoeing and hand pulling will be necessary.

Possible problems Carrot fly, specific to carrots and parsnips, is the only major pest, although wireworm also attack the roots in new gardens or on ground that was old grassland. Soil insecticide (bromophos or diazinon) in the seed drill and applied around the crowns of the plants once or twice while they are growing, is the most effective control. Screening the plants to prevent access to the flies, intersowing with a disguising crop (see page 24) and resettling by watering in after thinning out are the natural

alternatives to using insecticides.

Culturally, by sowing maincrop carrots at the end of May and always lifting earlies by the end of August, you will avoid the pests' main egg-laying periods and any ensuing problems.

Growing time 80 days for short-rooted and 130 days for intermediate- and long-rooted varieties.

Harvesting Pull early carrots from June, using a fork to lever them from the soil without damage. Lift the maincrop from August to October or, in milder areas on light soil, leave them in the ground for the winter protected by straw and polythene sheeting. Roots for storage in boxes of peat or sand are lifted between October and December. Only firm, undamaged crops should be stored and they must be examined regularly through the winter for signs of rot.

Special points Sowing sparsely reduces labour, reduces thinning, reduces the smell of bruised plants and thus their attraction to passing carrot flies. If thinning has to be done, choose a dull or wet evening, dispose of the thinnings in the dustbin or bonfire and firm and water in the remaining seedlings.

Varieties Short-rooted – 'Early Nantes': a slightly tapered, tender, early favourite. 'Kundulus': a small ball-rooted, fast growing, early cropper, with a shape and length that probably makes it the best for shallow soils. Intermediate-rooted – 'Nantes Tip Top': an evenly tapering, cylinder-shaped carrot; clean and core-free flesh, which makes it excellent for eating. 'Royal Chantenay': a selection of the popular 'Chantenay Red Cored'. Long-rooted – 'Autumn King': a very long-rooted but stumpy late variety good for storing over the winter.

CAULIFLOWER

A hardy, single-flowering head type of brassica. Like cabbage, the different varieties give a long cropping season, but its scarce gap is usually mid winter. It can spread up to 1·2 m (4 ft) wide. The mid winter gap and the time and space taken, the difficulty and unpredictability of growing the crop, all reduce its value in a small garden.

Soil The soil must have adequate organic manure to help conserve water.

Sowing and planting Rows, 15 cm

To grow cauliflowers successfully, you must have deep rich soil, follow planting instructions carefully and water well. They can be tricky plants to cultivate.

(6 in) apart. Seeds, 13 mm ($\frac{1}{2}$ in) deep, not less than 13 mm ($\frac{1}{2}$ in) apart. Remove the weakest seedlings as they grow to leave transplants about 7·5 cm (3 in) apart when ready for moving. Sow all types between mid March and May. Grow the seedlings on until they are quite large plants with at least six leaves before carefully transplanting with as large a root system and as much soil as possible. Plant firmly between June and July.

Allow one plant per sq m (sq yd).

Cultivation Keeping the soil moist at all times is the main secret of success.

Seedlings and mature plants forming curds are most susceptible to water shortage. Mulching helps a great deal. It is a hungry crop; liquid feeding at the roots, and foliar feeding until the curd forms, will both help to ensure a much better crop.

Consult brassicas (see pages 46 to 47) for points on general cultivation.

Possible problems Premature formation of small curds is caused by lack of water and browning of the curds by either sun scorch or frost damage. Protect from both these problems by bending the outer leaves over the centre.

Growing time 150–350 days.

Harvesting Cut the heads progressively as required, while still tight and firm. Do not leave until the flower heads begin to separate. Plants pulled complete with roots and hung up will keep some weeks in a cool place.

Varieties Summer: 'All The Year Round' must be the first choice as it is

Celeriac is a good speciality vegetable to try, as it is fairly easy to grow. The edible root has a delicious nutty flavour.

Possible problems One or two carrot or celery pests occasionally cause problems but, apart from slugs, celeriac is remarkably trouble-free.

Growing time 220 days.

Harvesting Lift at any time, but the roots increase in flavour with size, so they are normally grown on until October before harvesting begins. Not altogether hardy but it can stay in the ground with some protection in most areas. In cold, heavy soil lift and store in boxes of peat.

Varieties 'Claudia': the best as it combines the flavour and solid storage qualities of 'Marble Ball' with a less lumpy exterior – a considerable bonus.

CELERY

A member of the carrot family and originally a native of marshland, celery is a biennial grown for harvesting in its first year. In spite of its value as both a cooked and raw vegetable, it is such a complicated and time-consuming crop that you will need to be keen in order to grow it. The self-blanching types are a little easier, however, and, luckily, most commercially grown celery is now self-blanching.

Soil Rich, well prepared soil with plenty of organic manure is preferred by both types of celery. The trench for trench varieties should be 30 cm (12 in) deep and 38 cm (15 in) wide. Dig over the bottom as in double digging and add a generous layer of manure or compost. Tread this down well before returning the top soil, firming to within about 7·5 cm (3 in) of the trench top. The remaining soil from the trench is ridged along the sides to be used later in earthing-up the plants as they grow.

If the plants are to be grown on the level, using blanching collars, prepare the trench in the same way but completely fill it with top soil.

Sowing and planting Sow thinly under glass in trays or pots, in early March in a heated greenhouse or propagator; April in a cold greenhouse or frame. Transplant into deeper trays when seedlings have two true leaves. Gradually

probably the easiest; 'Snow Crown', an F1 hybrid produces firm, round, medium-weight heads. Autumn: 'Barrier Reef' is a newer variety recommended for its good leaf cover, which protects the curd (flower) from browning frost. Winter: the so-called winter varieties actually grow through the winter and are cut in the spring, so the name is a little misleading; they are not totally hardy and even the various strains of 'English Winter', such as 'St George', are really only possible in very mild areas.

CELERIAC

Turnip-rooted celery is much less labour intensive and somewhat easier to grow than celery. It has an attractive and distinctive nutty flavour and it does not have the problem of stringiness as it ages. In spite of these assets, however, celeriac is still a rarity in the vegetable plot.

Soil Soil type and conditions preferred are rich and well prepared with lots of organic manure if possible.

Sowing and planting Sow two seeds to a peat pot, under glass no later than February or March. Remove the weaker seedling as soon as possible to avoid disturbing the remaining one. Grow seedlings on until they have about six leaves and harden off before planting out in late May or early June.

Plant 30 cm (12 in) apart in rows 45 cm (18 in) apart.

Cultivation Keep well-watered for maximum growth and final size, but dry conditions do not affect flavour or texture to any degree. Keep the 'bulb' sides free of leaves and shoots as the summer progresses. Earthing-up from September protects the roots in cold areas.

harden off when seedlings have more than five leaves.

The self-blanching varieties should be planted in blocks of short rows at 23 cm (9 in) spacing in both directions. For details of the trench for those varieties requiring this, see below. Plant 23 cm (9 in) apart. Allow 10 plants per sq m (sq yd) for the trench varieties and 15 for the self-blanching ones.

Cultivation Lack of water for any length of time causes plants to bolt and makes their heart stems inedible. The manure in the trench will help to conserve water, but in dry weather 20 litres per sq m (3¾ gallons per sq yd) will be needed to top up the soil water reserve.

When self-blanching plants are well established, it is best if straw or some similar material is pushed in around the sides to assist with blanching both the inner and outer stems. Trench celery will need its first earthing-up when it is about 30 cm (12 in) high. First, tie the stems loosely together and then, in three equal stages of about 7·5 cm (3 in) each at roughly three-week intervals, earth-up to the bottom of the leaves. Using blanching collars of paper, corrugated card or polythene avoids the necessity of earthing-up.

A row of trench-grown celery which has been earthed-up.

Possible problems The maggots of celery fly tunnel inside the leaves, causing blistering. Affected plants may die, but in any case the stems will be bitter tasting. Picking off affected leaves will be successful if caught early enough, but using unblistered plants and spraying, if necessary, with a short-lived systemic insecticide, like permethrin and heptenophos, is the only real answer.

Slugs are the biggest problem on both types of celery, particularly when they get inside the blanching collars. Slug tape, encircling each plant, is probably the best deterrent.

Growing time Self-blanching 150 days; trench 250 days.

Harvesting Cut self-blanching varieties as needed from mid to late July. Trench varieties are usually ready by November, but the pink types are slightly hardier and can be left until December or January. Freezing destroys the crispness of celery but it still maintains its flavour for cooking. Scrub and blanch for about three minutes.

Special points Older seeds are known to germinate better than fresh ones. To ensure that as many as possible grow, fluid drilling of pre-germinated seed (see page 32) is particularly valuable.

Varieties Self-blanching varieties – 'Latham Self-blanching': resistant to running to seed. 'Greensnap': stringless. Trench types – 'Hopkins Fenlander': excellent flavour and crispness, but not easy to grow well. 'Clayworth Prize Pink': naturally pale pink, but blanches easily.

CHICORY

Belonging to the daisy family, chicory is

TRENCH-GROWN CELERY

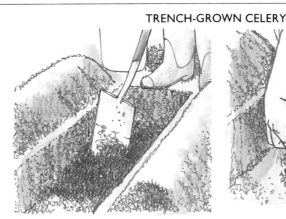

1. Dig a trench about 30 cm (12 in) deep and 38 cm (15 in) wide. Loosen the bottom of the trench to another spade's depth and add manure.

2. Tread down the trench bottom. Return the topsoil and firm to within 7·5 cm (3 in) of top. Ridge remaining soil along the trench edge.

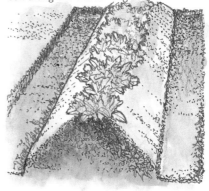

3. When the celery reaches 30 cm (12 in) high, loosely tie black polythene or newspaper around the plants.

4. Earthing-up is done in three stages, at three weekly intervals. After last earthing-up, only leaves should be visible.

Two varieties of chicory: 'Normato' (left) and 'Sugar Loaf' (right).

grown for its lettuce-like leaves or, the forcing varieties for their blanched shoots or 'chicons'. It is more bitter than lettuce and not to everyone's taste, but the chicons are less bitter, much crisper and make a useful contribution to salads.

Site and soil Grow in any ordinary soil in an open, sunny place.

Sowing and planting Sow the seed of forcing varieties in May and June, the non-forcing varieties in June and July. Sow thinly 13 mm ($\frac{1}{2}$ in) deep in rows 30 cm (12 in) apart.

Thin out the seedlings to 15 cm (6 in) and then, for the non-forcing types only, to 30 cm (12 in).

Cultivation Keep down the weeds by hoeing, and water in dry conditions. Lift the thick roots of the forcing varieties in November, cut the leaves back to about 2.5 cm (1 in) and the roots to about 15 cm (6 in).

Pot them tightly in pots or boxes of peat or sand with the leaf crowns just showing, and keep them covered or in the dark. Also

FORCING CHICORY

1. Lift forcing varieties of chicory in November. With a sharp knife, cut the leaves back to 2.5 cm (1 in) and the roots to about 15 cm (6 in).

2. Pot the chicory tightly in pots of sand or peat, so that their leaf crowns are just showing above the surface.

3. Place an empty pot, with its drainage holes covered by black plastic, over the chicory crowns to keep them in the dark.

4. Maintain a temperature of about 13°C (55°F) around the chicory. They are ready for cutting when they reach 15 cm (6 in) high.

keep them warm – about 13°C (55°F), to encourage new growth which forms the chicons.

Possible problems Watch for slugs, and it is a good idea to use a pesticide such as bromophos, raked into the soil before sowing, to combat any soil pests.

Growing time 130–200 days.

Harvesting Cut the non-forcing chicory during October to December. The heads will store quite well in a cool place or, in milder areas, they can be left in the ground, provided they are protected well from severe frost.

The chicons from the forced varieties will be ready for cutting in about four weeks when they are about 15 cm (6 in) high. Cut the chicons just above the top of their roots and return them to the dark to produce a second crop of smaller chicons. As the chicons easily turn bitter in the light even after they have been cut, keep them in the dark.

Varieties 'Sugar Loaf': a good, reliable non-forcing variety. 'Whitloof': the most popular for forcing. 'Normato': a newer variety that naturally produces tighter chicons.

CUCUMBER

Varieties suitable for growing outdoors are often called ridge cucumbers because

Outdoor cucumbers will reach about 15–20 cm (6–8 in) long. Harvesting before they reach their full size will encourage more fruiting.

they used to be grown on ridges of loam or compost. Nowadays, however, they are cultivated in pockets of rich soil. Though they can be grown outdoors in most parts of the country, they do require a sunny site sheltered from cold winds.

Soil Dig holes 30 cm (1 ft) deep and 30 cm (1 ft) across leaving a 60–90 cm (2–3 ft) gap between them. Fill with a mixture of rotted organic matter and potting compost. Cover with low mounds of the topsoil.

Sowing and planting Indoors: in spring sow seed in peat pots filled with seed compost, allowing two to three seeds per pot. Germinate at a temperature of 21°C (70°F). When large enough to handle, thin, leaving only the strongest seedlings. Harden off and plant out in May to June. Outdoors: in May sow seed in planting pockets. Protect with cloches until June.

Cultivation When seven leaves appear, pinch out the growing tip. Support with wire or canes or allow it to trail along

---

GROWING OUTDOOR CUCUMBERS

Make planting pockets for the cucumbers by digging square holes 30 cm (12 in) deep and across. Fill with manure or compost and cover with a low heap of topsoil.

When seven leaves have formed on each young plant, pinch out the growing tip. This encourages the side shoots – which will bear fruit – to develop.

Any side shoots which do not have flowers when their seventh leaf forms, should have their tips pinched out.

ground. Pinch out the tips of side shoots without flowers at the seventh leaf. Water around the plants in dry weather.

Cover the soil with polythene when fruit forms, and feed with a liquid tomato fertilizer when the fruit starts swelling.

Possible problems Aphids and diseases such as cucumber mosaic, grey mould and powdery mildew.

Growing time 85–100 days.

Harvesting Cut with a sharp knife before fruits reach maximum size – when about 15–20 cm (6–8 in) long.

Special points By picking the cucumbers before they reach full size, you will encourage further fruiting on the plants.

Varieties 'Burpless Tasty Green': an F1 hybrid resistant to mildew, producing tender-skinned fruit. 'Chinese Long Green': a hardy early variety giving a good crop. 'King of Ridge': reliable, hardy and produces a tasty crop. 'Tokyo Slicer': a vigorous heavy cropping hybrid with an especially good flavour.

ENDIVE

Closely related to chicory, endive is grown as an annual for its lettuce-like leaves. It should always be blanched before picking to counteract its naturally bitter taste. There are two basic types: those with curly leaves, sometimes called staghorns, and those with broad, plain leaves, generally called Batavian. The former will provide a summer and autumn crop, while the latter, which are hardier, can be used during the winter.

Soil Well drained, with plenty of organic material dug in during the autumn and a dressing of general fertilizer before sowing.

Sowing and planting Sow thinly in rows 30 cm (12 in) apart in drills 13 mm ($\frac{1}{2}$ in) deep. Progressively thin seedlings after two true leaves have appeared until the curly-leaved varieties are 23 cm (9 in) apart and the broad-leaved ones 30 cm (12 in) apart. If necessary the thinnings can be transplanted. Sow the curly-leaved

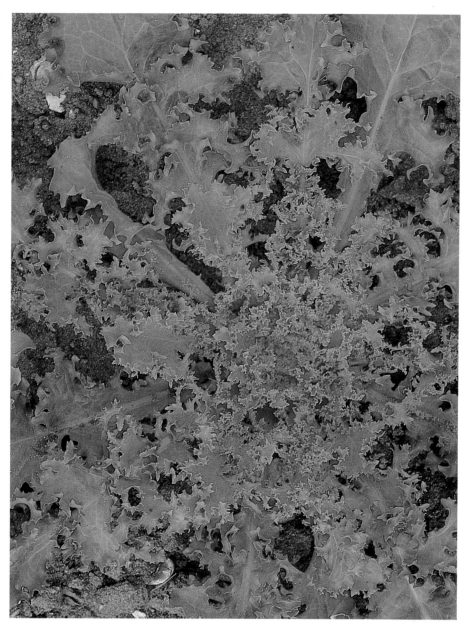

endive successively during March to August and the Batavian type during July to September.

Allow 12 curly-leaved plants per sq m (sq yd) and eight broad-leaved plants per sq m (sq yd).

Cultivation Keep watered in dry weather and keep down weeds by regular hoeing. Liquid feed during the growing season to ensure good leaf development.

Possible problems Comparatively trouble-free, but greenfly and slugs can both be a nuisance and should be controlled by the usual remedial measures.

Running to seed or bolting must be avoided by correct watering during dry periods.

Growing time 100–140 days.

Harvesting Some two to three weeks before picking in later summer, or five weeks before picking in winter, you will need to commence the blanching operation. This will be approximately three months after sowing. First, ensure that the plants you want are thoroughly dry – if necessary cover the cloches a little earlier. Second, loosely tie up the leaves with garden string, and then cover the plant with a suitable-sized flower pot, covering its drainage holes with tiles or black plastic to exclude the light. Only blanch the plants you require for immediate use, for they soon rot once blanched.

Special points   The winter-picked broad-leaved types will need the protection of cloches in very cold districts.

Varieties Curly-leaved – 'Green Curled': pretty, deeply cut, crisp leaves good for picking in late summer and autumn. 'Moss Curled': much the same. Broad-leaved – 'Batavian Green': for late autumn and winter picking. 'Golda': a newish compact variety with slightly upright leaves for easier blanching.

FENNEL, FLORENCE

The ferny leaved fennel, a member of the carrot family, is usually grown as a herb, but the Florence form has a bulbous base which, like its foliage, has the flavour of aniseed. It can be eaten raw, boiled, steamed or braised.

Site and soil   It requires a well drained, light, fertile soil and a sunny sheltered position if the bulb is to form.

Sowing Sow seed thinly in April, 13 mm ($\frac{1}{2}$ in) deep and in rows 45 cm (18 in) apart. Thin the seedlings to about 30 cm (12 in) apart.

Cultivation Keep well watered and feed regularly to ensure rapid and even growth. Ridge the soil around the base as it begins to swell in order to blanch the 'bulb', and continue this until it is fully swollen, about 10 cm (4 in) across.

Allow eight plants per sq m (sq yd).

Possible problems Running to seed or bolting will be caused by a check in growth due to insufficient watering. Watch out for slugs and snails.

Growing time   80 days.

Harvesting   The bulbous base is ready for cutting through the summer and, in good years, through to early autumn if it is protected. Cut the bulb off just above ground level when it is the size of a tennis ball.

Special points Warm summers are needed for this crop so, in this country, an open south-facing position which receives plent of sun and is sheltered from cold wind, is essential.

Varieties   'Zefo Fino': is a popular bolt-resistant variety.

KALE

Kale, a member of the cabbage family, is valuable for its hardiness and its winter-picking season. It is reasonably easy to grow and, picked young, the leaves, although stronger tasting than many brassicas, make an excellent vegetable.

Soil Kale will grow on any well drained ordinary soil provided it is reasonably firm. Lime may be necessary if the soil is at all acid.

Opposite: Curly-leaved varieties of endive are sown in spring and summer for cutting in summer and autumn. They have a slightly bitter taste which makes them an interesting alternative to lettuce in salads.

Florence Fennel 'Zefo Fino', grown for its swollen bulb-like base which tastes of aniseed, is only worth cultivating in the mildest parts of the country. The soil should be well drained, light and fertile and the site should be sunny.

Kale is an easy vegetable to grow as it is extremely hardy, will tolerate poor soil and is unaffected by the usual brassica problems: cabbage root fly, club root and pigeons.

Sowing and planting Sow the seed thinly in April or May, in drills 13 mm ($\frac{1}{2}$ in) deep and in rows 15 cm (6 in) apart. Thin the seedlings to 7·5 cm (3 in) apart and grow them on strongly until they are ready for transplanting at about 15 cm (6 in) high.

Water the rows before lifting and plant out firmly and deeply from late June to early August, 45 cm (18 in) apart between plants and rows. Water in well.

Allow four plants per sq m (sq yd).

Cultivation Ensure that the plants are firmly in the soil. Keep down weeds, and water in dry weather. The taller varieties may need staking to prevent wind rock.

Possible problems The pests and diseases which afflict other brassicas seldom affect kale. The caterpillars of the cabbage white butterfly may attack young plants. Hand picking the caterpillars is the easiest remedy.

Growing time 200–250 days.

Harvesting Pick only the youngest leaves, from the centres first, starting in late autumn. Picking stimulates the pro-duction of further tender shoots, but do not strip the plants.

Varieties 'Dwarf Green Curled': a smaller variety that does not require staking. 'Pentland Brig': less curly and its immature flowers can be used as if they were broccoli.

KOHL RABI

Kohl rabi is a swollen-stemmed brassica with a taste of mild cabbage – a delicate nutty flavour and a smooth texture when eaten young and small.

Soil A firm, fertile, well manured soil with adequate lime, in a sunny position is ideal for kohl rabi.

Sowing Sow seed thinly at three-week intervals from April to August, 13 mm ($\frac{1}{2}$ in) deep, in rows 30 cm (12 in) apart. Thin the seedlings gradually until 15 cm (6 in) apart. Do not transplant, and keep well watered.

Allow 18 plants per sq m (sq yd).

Cultivation Weed regularly and keep protected from birds.

Possible problems The usual brassica troubles are uncommon because kohl rabi grows so quickly.

Growing time 56–80 days

Harvesting Begin picking when the stems are no bigger than a hen's egg. This should be in July, from April-sown seed, to November or December, from July-sown seed. They do not store: eat them straight from the ground.

Varieties 'Green Vienna', 'White Vienna' and 'Purple Vienna': skins of those colours, but all have white flesh and are equally good.

LEEK

This mild member of the onion family, grown for its white base, is very hardy and thus a welcome winter vegetable. While it has a long growing season, its relatively high yield from a small area makes it an excellent crop.

Soil Any good, ordinary soil with reasonable drainage and sufficient humus will grow healthy leeks. Spread manure or compost the previous autumn, or dig in well rotted organic matter before planting.

Sowing and planting Rows 15 cm (6 in) apart. Sow seeds 13 mm ($\frac{1}{2}$ in) deep, thinly and evenly along the drill. Under glass (heated or cloches): February or March. Outdoors: March or April, or June for late cropping. Thin seedlings to 4 cm ($1\frac{1}{2}$ in) apart in rows.

Plant maincrop between June and August, earlier in the north, later in the south; May planting will give smaller and earlier leeks. Plant in rows 30 cm (12 in) apart with 15 cm (6 in) between plants. Select the best and largest seedlings, trim the roots and shorten the leaves by half. Make holes 20 cm (8 in) deep with a dibber and drop one plant in each, pour in water to puddle-in the plant and leave it to grow. The deep hole will encourage a longer white stem as the surrounding soil gradually falls in.

Allow 18 plants per sq m (sq yd).

Cultivation Leeks do not usually need much water, but keep the soil evenly

Leeks take up relatively little room and have a high yield, so they make excellent winter vegetables for a small plot.

Kohl rabi are not suitable for storing; eat them soon after harvesting. Though the root is usually used, it is possible to boil the young leaves, treating them like spinach.

moist, and mulch and water thoroughly in dry weather.

Allow the planting hole to fill with soil naturally, and gradually earth up to increase the blanched-stem length. Keep soil away from the leaf crown and trim back leaves if they touch the ground. Regular liquid feeding when the plants are growing strongly will increase the girth of the stems. but do not use high-nitrogen fertilizer after August.

Possible problems   Fortunately, leeks are largely free of pests and diseases. Stem and bulb eelworm can cause distorted stems and leaves, but this is more common in onions. Rust, on the other hand, is more of a problem on leeks. There is no treatment for either bulb eelworm or rust, other than burning the affected plants and not growing this crop on the same soil for as long as possible.

Growing time   Early and mid season types, 200 days; late types, 300 days.

Harvesting   Early types: September to November; mid season types: December to January; late types: March to May or even June.

Early varieties tend not to be so hardy and should be used before winter sets in. Mid- and late-season types are perfectly happy left in the soil through the winter and, to release the ground for spring planting, they can be lifted and temporarily heeled-in in a spare corner of the vegetable patch.

Special points   Their extensive, thick fibrous roots make leeks good soil improvers and thus good starter crops on newly dug land.

Varieties   Early type – 'Walton Mammoth': an excellent culinary and show variety. Mid-season type – 'Musselburgh': a hardy and reliable favourite. Late type – 'Winter Crop': the flavour of 'Musselburgh' and even hardier.

LETTUCE

Lettuce will grow in most soils and most gardens. Sown under glass (for transplanting outdoors) or outdoors in succession over spring and summer, it can provide you with a regular supply of fresh leaves.

Soil   Fertile well-drained soil. Not too acid and kept moist. Dig compost or well-rotted manure into soil in autumn or winter. Before sowing or planting rake to fine tilth and apply general fertilizer.

Sowing and planting   Indoors: sow in trays or small compost-filled peat pots, two seeds per pot. Thin out leaving the stronger seedlings. Harden off and transplant outdoors, setting 30 cm (12 in) apart in rows. Outdoors: from March to July, sow seed thinly in shallow furrows 10 mm ($\frac{1}{2}$ in) deep and 30 cm (12 in) apart. Alternatively, you can buy strips of young plants and plant them in rows as above.

Cultivation   Water well, and keep down weeds between rows with a hoe.

Possible problems   Protect seedlings from birds and slugs. Greenfly and grey mould can affect the crop, and they may bolt if short of water or overcrowded.

Growing time   For butterhead and cos varieties, 56–100 days; Crisphead varieties, 56–100 days; Loose leaf varieties, 42–56 days.

Harvesting   Pick when a firm heart has formed. Cut with a knife or pull up the entire plant. Leaves of loose leaf varieties can be picked off when required.

Special points   Lettuces are suitable for intercropping: grow between rows of

Loose leaf lettuce varieties such as 'Salad Bowl' and 'Red Salad Bowl' do not have a heart. The leaves are picked a few at a time, with the plant remaining in the ground – and productive – for several weeks.

'Webb's Wonderful', with its large, firm heart, is one of the most popular crisphead lettuces.

A spring crop of butterhead lettuces, started off under cloches.

slower growing vegetables or with ornamental garden plants.

Varieties Butterhead – 'All Year Round' suitable for sowing all year around, unlikely to bolt. 'Buttercrunch': a summer cropper with a compact crunchy heart of creamy leaves. 'May Queen': early summer variety with red-tinged leaves. 'Tom Thumb': early summer variety which matures quickly and has fine flavour, compact and good for small plot. Cos – 'Little Gem': quick maturing and compact early summer cropper with a sweet flavour. 'Lobjoits Green': large deep green very crisp leaves, early summer variety. 'Paris White': large pale green, crisp, variety, for summer cropping. Crisphead – 'Iceberg': crisp, white-hearted lettuce for spring and summer sowing. 'Webbs Wonderful': large-hearted lettuce for summer cropping, succeeds in hot weather. 'Windermere': sow under glass or outdoors for early summer crop, quick maturing and fine head. Loose leaf – 'Salad Bowl': cut and curled leaves which can be regularly picked off plant. 'Red Salad Bowl': reddish-brown leaves for regularly picking off plant, summer cropper.

MARROW, COURGETTE, PUMPKIN AND SQUASH

These are all frost-tender annuals belonging to the cucumber family. Courgettes are simply young marrows; pumpkins and squashes are the American counterparts. They all take up a lot of room during the heaviest cropping season and, although courgettes can be prolific producers, the low number of fruits cut make them only really worthwhile in a large garden.

Soil Any good soil enriched with compost or manure will grow satisfactory marrows, etc, but for large crops the traditional marrow mound or pit is still probably the best way. A 30 cm (12 in) cube is dug out, the soil from it mixed with an equal volume of well rotted manure or compost, and the hole refilled with this, leaving a low mound on which the seedlings or seeds are planted.

Sowing and planting Under glass: sow two seeds, not before April, in 7·5 cm (3 in) pots of peat-based compost and keep warm. As soon as true leaves appear between the seed leaves (cotyledons) pull out the weaker ones. Outdoors: sow *in situ* in early June or when all danger of frost is past. Use the same procedure as under glass.

These vegetables are all very cold-sensitive; do not plant out the seedlings until after the last frost. This is usually June, but recent years have been much colder and there are always exceptionally cold areas. Set the plants deeply – they will root from their stems – which will help to prevent wind rock. Leave a shallow saucer-shaped depression around the plant to assist watering.

Allow one to two plants per sq m (sq yd).

Cultivation Water copiously throughout the summer. Mulch around plants to conserve water and to keep the fruits clean. Feed continuously with a high-potash soluble fertilizer, such as Phostrogen, or liquid seaweed. Pinch out the tips of trailing varieties.

Possible problems. Many of the problems which afflict cucumbers could affect this group, but this is not generally so. Apart from slugs, the only common problem is likely to be cucumber mosaic virus, which causes patterning and stunting of the leaves and fruit. As aphids are carriers of this virus, the plants will have to be destroyed to prevent its spread.

Growing time 80–120 days.

Harvesting Pick courgettes frequently as soon as they are 7·5–10 cm (3–4 in) long to keep them forming. This will start about mid July. The mature fruits of marrows, squashes and pumpkins will not be ready until a little later but they can be picked and eaten at any size. For winter storage the fruits must thoroughly ripen on the plant before picking.

Special points Bees and other insects normally pollinate the flowers outdoors, but in cool or overcast weather they may need assistance. To hand pollinate, take off an open male flower, which is the one with pollen and without a tiny fruit behind it, remove the petals if it helps and then simply rub it into the centre of the female

'Vegetable Spaghetti' so-named because of spaghetti-like strands which form inside the fruit when it is boiled, is a variety of squash.

Marrows, frost-tender vegetables grown in the summer, take up considerable space – they are only worth considering in a large vegetable garden.

Opposite: 'Green Bush' is an FI hybrid which can be treated as a courgette (cut the small fruits), or as a marrow (leave the fruits to mature).

Opposite: 'Atlantic Giant', a pumpkin renowned for its record-breaking size and excellent flavour.

flowers, the ones with a tiny swollen fruit behind them.

Varieties Marrow – 'Green Bush': the most compact, ideal for small gardens. Courgette – 'Aristocrat': for earliness and high yield. 'Gold Rush': for colour and flavour. Pumpkin – 'Atlantic Giant': not only the biggest, it also has the most flavour. Squash – 'Vegetable Spaghetti' is fun and quite tasty; spaghetti-like flesh. Custard marrows are more attractive than useful except for wine making.

ONION AND SHALLOT

The leaf-like layers of onions show that they are bulbs and, apart from the leek, they are the only true bulbs grown for eating in this country. Onions are also unique in being grown from both seed and sets (small immature bulbs). Shallots divide to produce a clump of small bulbs from a single full-sized bulb while spring onions are grown from seed. Alternatively use the thinnings from bulb varieties, as spring onions for salads. Whether from seed or sets, they are a good value crop.

Soil Onions will grow perfectly well in any good garden soil with sufficient organic content. Sets will tolerate less fertile conditions and less humus in the soil than seed-raised plants.

Sowing and planting Rows, 23 cm (9 in) apart. Sow seed 13 mm ($\frac{1}{2}$ in) deep, very thinly, no less than 6 mm ($\frac{1}{4}$ in) apart; Japanese seed, 25 mm (1 in) apart. Remove weakest gradually until they are finally 10 cm (4 in) apart. Under glass: sow in December, traditionally Boxing Day, or into January. Plant out in April. Outdoors: sow in February and March, or August for late sown and Japanese varieties.

Before sowing or planting, fertilize the soil and rake over it when dry. Stamp down the soil and rake the ground again to ensure a fine surface.

Plant sets in rows 23 cm (9 in) apart, with sets 10 cm (4 in) apart. Trim off tips before planting, and plant firmly with tip just showing to help deter birds pulling them up.

Allow 80 bulbs per sq m (sq yd).

Cultivation Keep soil moist and mulch

to conserve water. Water only in very dry weather and not at all as the bulbs ripen.

Such a low-growing crop is very susceptible to being swamped by weeds. Hoe carefully, preferably with the traditional short-handled onion hoe. When the leaves fall over naturally to herald the start of ripening, deliberately bend them down away from the direction of the sun. Pulling soil away from the crowns and sides of the bulbs will also assist ripening.

Possible problems Birds may pull out sets. The onion fly lays eggs in the soil and the grubs eat into the base of the bulb. Dress seed bed with bromophos or diazinon or use sets which are not affected. Premature running to seed can be caused by planting too early in cold years. The larger sets aggravate this problem, so select small firm ones, no larger than 20 mm ($\frac{3}{4}$ in) across. Pick off any flower heads and use these bulbs as soon as possible. Bullneck, a distinct thickening of the bulb at the point where the leaves start, is the result of too much softening nitrogen fertilizer or too much manure. Feed with a high-potash soluble feed until the bulbs stop swelling.

Growing time Spring-sown seed, 150 days; autumn-sown, 300 days. Sets, 150 days. Shallots, 130 days.

Harvesting Autumn-sown and Japanese onions are ready for harvesting about June. Spring-sown seed and sets will be ready from about August onwards. Thinnings may be used as salad onions. Use any bolted (those with flowers) or bullneck onions first. About two weeks after the bulbs have had the soil pulled away from them they can be carefully lifted and laid out to dry in the sun.

For storing, onions must be thoroughly ripened and very firm. Japanese onions do not keep well. Store others in plaited ropes or in the legs of old tights, with a knot between each bulb. The next one up will not then fall out when the bottom one is cut off for use.

Varieties Seed – 'Ailsa Craig': still the favourite globe-shaped bulb. 'Bedfordshire Champion': a large, round onion, similar to 'Ailsa Craig' but can be stored for longer. Downy mildew is frequently a

As soon as the onion leaves start to fall over, bend them towards the ground and away from the sun to encourage the bulbs to ripen.

Below: For each shallot set planted, 8–12 similar-sized bulbs will be produced in a cluster in the summer. When the leaves turn yellow, usually in July, lift and separate the clusters of bulbs.

'Brunswick', a medium-sized onion with a mild flavour, is grown from seed. It has excellent keeping qualities.

'White Lisbon' is a quick growing spring onion suitable for sowing in succession.

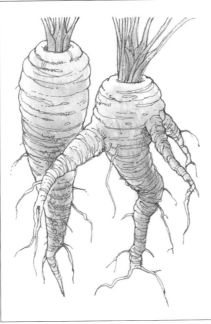

Parsnips grown on over manured soil may develop forked roots.

problem. 'Reliance': flat bulbs, stores well, good for autumn sowing in warmer areas. 'Imai Yellow': hardier Japanese variety, medium, flat bulb for autumn sowing. Sets – 'Sturon': globe-shaped, does not easily run to seed and very large. 'Rijnsburger': the best for storage. 'Unwins First Early': for autumn planting. Shallots – 'Hative de Niort': mild. 'The Aristocrat': for quantity. 'Paris Silver Skin' or 'Barletta': for pickling. Spring onions – 'White Lisbon': quick growing with a mild flavour. 'Ishikura': straight sided and does not form bulbs.

PARSNIP

A biennial root crop used in its first year before flowering. In the same family as the carrot, but a quite different vegetable with a distinct flavour which is not always appreciated.

Soil Deep, full-bodied soil, without fresh manure, is best but they will grow perfectly well on any reasonable soil.

Sowing and planting Rows 30 cm (12 in). Sow seed 13 mm ($\frac{1}{2}$ in) deep, 15 cm (6 in) apart in threes. For even, long straight roots, sow in deep conical holes made with a dibber or stick and filled with sieved soil or loam-based seed compost, at the same spacings. This is a particularly good method on shallow soils. Sowing seed from late February to April is the normal recommendation, but recent trials have shown that later sowing, until June, still produces a satisfactory, if slightly smaller, crop.

Like most root crops, parsnips are not usually transplanted but sowing in tall sweet pea tubes and transplanting these whole, without disturbing the roots, is successful and allows earlier sowing in warmer conditions and an earlier crop. Fluid drilling is also useful since the main reason for sowing three seeds at each growing position is that parsnips germinate erratically.

Allow 20 plants per sq m (sq yd).

Cultivation Overwet conditions encourage canker but this is a deep-rooted crop so you will only need to water in a drought. Weed carefully; damage to the root crown increases the risk of canker.

Above: To grow long, straight-rooted parsnips, sow the seed in a deep, conical hole filled with fine, sieved soil or a loam-based seed compost.

Possible problems Canker is a disease specific to parsnips and is usually worse on acid soil with too much humus. Sowing too early in cold, wet soil aggravates the condition. Liming and choosing a resistant variety helps prevent it.

Growing time 250 days.

Harvesting Parsnips are ready from a normal sowing by about early November, but as they are perfectly hardy in all but the most severe winters, they may be left in the ground and used as required. There is nothing to stop you digging young, immature roots before the main season, but this crop is the one proven case of frost actually improving its flavour. Lift carefully with a fork. Unless the space is required, there is no point in freezing them although they freeze quite well if cubed and blanched for five minutes.

Special points As parsnip seed rapidly deteriorates, always use fresh seed from sealed foil packets.

Varieties 'Tender and True': good for flavour, reliability and size. 'White Gem'; shorter, with excellent flavour and resistance to canker.

PEA

An annual legume, peas are the most popular vegetables for eating whether canned or frozen – but with the home gardener they take second place to their cousins the broad, runner and French beans. In fact, although freshly picked garden peas are superior in flavour, this is the only advantage they have for they are not superior in nutritional value.

Soil For a worthwhile crop the soil needs to be very deep and fertile. Deep digging and plenty of organic manure, at least 12 kg per sq m (25 lb per sq yd) are indispensable. Lime should be used to keep the soil neutral to slightly alkaline.

Sowing Pea varieties are quite variable in height – from 'Meteor', a round-seeded

Right: 'Bikini', a pea bred for easier picking since it has fewer leaves and more tendrils than most peas.

early at about 30 cm (12 in), to 'Alderman', a maincrop at about 1·5 m (5 ft). The distance between the rows should be the same as the variety's ultimate height. It is a good idea to consider growing the taller varieties up leaning wire-covered frames as these will make the best use of the space and deter weeds between rows. Seeds should be sown about 5 cm (2 in) deep, with 7·5 cm (3 in) between them, in three staggered rows in 15 cm (6 in) wide, flat-bottomed drills.

Under glass (cloches): hardier, round-seeded varieties can be sown in October or November, in warmer areas, or February and March in colder ones, for an earlier crop. Outdoors: sow every three weeks from April to June for successional crops.

Allow 30–40 plants per sq m (sq yd).

Cultivation Lack of water could prevent pods swelling, but this is not common since peas only suffer in very dry weather. Mulching will probably be sufficient protection.

Nitrogenous fertilizer is not usually beneficial and may be harmful, but one or two extra feeds of liquid potash fertilizer will increase the crop, especially if the weather is at all dry.

All varieties need protection and support. Two or three single strands of black cotton, not nylon thread, above the seed row will hinder birds. Shaking the seed in a little powdered seed dressing before sowing or stretching a renardine-soaked string along the soil surface, will both deter mice.

Late sowings will need the protection of cloches from August onwards if they are to crop reliably.

Possible problems Little maggots inside the pods are the tiny caterpillars of the pea moth. The only good prevention is a reasonably persistent spray such as dimethoate or fenitrothion. In cold, dry weather, mildew is quite common and, in addition to conserving water in the soil, an organic sulphur or triforine spray may be necessary.

Growing time Autumn-sown, about 200 days; spring-sown, about 100 days.

Harvesting The early sowings under cloches will be ready for picking from May

It is important to harvest peas regularly – if pods are allowed to mature for too long on the plant they will reduce its likely yield.

or June onwards; later sowings from July to September. Mangetout and petits pois about August.

Peas at their best are soft and sweet – when the pods are well rounded but not completely full. Test harvest one or two to make certain they are at their peak. Mangetout should be 7·5 cm (3 in) long and no more. Pick from the bottom of the plant upwards; do this regularly to keep them coming.

For freezing, shell, blanch for one minute and dry very thoroughly.

Dried peas must be left on the plant to ripen completely. In wet weather cut off the whole plant and hang up to dry in a cool place before shelling. After harvesting, cut off the dried tops and leave the roots in the soil to release their nitrogen.

Special points Support is essential; twiggy pea sticks must be pushed in on the rear side of the seedlings when they are no more than 7·5 cm (3 in) high or, for the taller varieties, use the pea frames mentioned earlier. Seedlings easily become damaged or eaten by slugs.

Until the pea plants meet between the rows, the spaces make ideal areas for intercropping salad crops.

Varieties First earlies – 'Feltham First': a round-seeded hardier type, 'Kelvedon Wonder': for successional sowing. Second Earlies – 'Onward': the usual choice. 'Bikini': has much reduced leaves and tendrils in their place which makes the pods easier to see and pick. Maincrop – 'Senator': both a heavy cropper and tasty. Mangetout (literally 'eat all') – 'Sugarsnap': the pods and the young peas are eaten without shelling; this variety is also useful for growing on as a maincrop. Petits pois are not simply baby peas but small

Early varieties of seed potato like 'Vanessa' should be sprouted before planting. Stand them, with their eyes uppermost, in shallow trays and keep in a cool, well lit place until 2·5 cm (1 in) long green sprouts appear.

Below: Brown patches on the foliage – the early signs of potato blight.

extra-sweet types, the best variety being 'Waverex'.

POTATO

A half-hardy perennial in the same family as the tomato, this familiar root crop is always referred to as a tuber, but is strictly an underground stem, as can be seen from its 'eyes' which are the buds that normally appear spaced up the stems of above-ground plants. The early (new) potatoes are worth growing, unless you have plenty of space for a quality maincrop variety.

Soil Any reasonable soil, well prepared, dug and manured the previous autumn, will raise a good crop. Never add lime as it encourages common scab disease.

Planting Potatoes are supplied as 'Certified Seed' (medium-sized potato 'sets', not real seed), which is raised under special disease-free conditions and certified by the Ministry of Agriculture as being pure and clean.

Plant earlies in rows 60 cm (2 ft) apart, the 'seed' 30 cm (12 in) apart, 10–15 cm (4–6 in) deep. Maincrop in rows 75 cm (30 in) apart, the 'seed' 38 cm (15 in) apart, 10–15 cm (4–6 in) deep.

Sprouting seed potatoes before planting is vital for earlies and advisable for maincrop. Look for the eyes: most are towards the 'top' of the tuber and each has its 'eyebrow' underneath it. Stand the tubers, supported in damp peat if necessary, with their top ends uppermost, in shallow boxes – seed trays will do. Keep the trays in a well lit, cool place until firm, dark

green sprouts about 2·5 cm (1 in) long have formed from the upper eyes. This will take a month to six weeks if started in February, and they will then be ready for planting.

For a small supply of new potatoes at special times of the year, allow about twelve weeks before the special occasion and plant some tubers in pots or boxes in a greenhouse.

Allow about two to four plants per sq m (sq yd) of ground.

Cultivation The earthing-up and the plant's large leaf canopy conserve water effectively around the roots, but once the tubers begin to form, right through to harvesting, it is vital not to allow the soil to dry out. Up to 20 litres per sq m (4 gallons per sq yd) every week may be necessary.

When the shoots are through the ground by about 23 cm (9 in), draw up the soil from the sides to make ridges around the bases of the plants. An alternative to this is to plant through black polythene sheeting – no earthing-up is then needed, weeds are effectively eliminated and the potatoes can be harvested a few at a time. The tubers form more or less on the surface and earthing-up is intended to keep them covered to prevent them greening (green tubers are mildly poisonous) and to encourage a larger crop. Polythene has both of these effects.

Possible problems Potato blight is the most serious disease; there is no cure, only prevention is possible. In warm

Left: By drawing soil into ridges around the base of potato plants when they are about 22 cm (9 in) tall, you help retain moisture around the roots.

Opposite: 'Desiree' is a popular maincrop variety easily distinguished by its pink flesh.

humid weather, soft brown patches appear on the leaves and later spread to the tubers. The only action is to watch the weather and the crop, and if blight is likely, spray with a copper fungicide or dithane. The odd infected plant must be pulled out and burned before the disease spreads to the others.

Flat, warty-like growths on the surface are usually common scab disease, but this is superficial and the crop is perfectly safe to eat provided you peel it first.

All plants that like a high-potash diet may show signs of magnesium deficiency from time to time, in yellowing on the older leaves between dark green veins. Epsom salts, 12·5 g per litre (2 oz per gallon) sprayed on the plants and soil will cure this. Alternatively, avoid the deficiency in the first place by feeding with a high-potash soluble fertilizer to which magnesium has been added.

Growing time Earlies, 100 days; maincrop, 150 days.

Harvesting Early potatoes are ready for lifting when their flowers open. Check a few plants first to see if they are a reasonable size. Dig them as required.

Maincrop are ready about two weeks after the foliage withers and dies – take it off as soon as this happens and leave the rows exposed until lifting. Use a flat-tined potato fork, keeping well back from the line of the row to avoid spearing the tubers. Always clear the ground completely of even the smallest tuber to prevent problems in the following year.

Special points Newly dug ground, especially old turf, will invariably be infested with wireworms which can easily ruin a potato crop. Dressing the soil with

'Wilja' is a reliable early potato with high yields and a reasonable flavour.

'Maris Piper' has high yields and good cooking qualities.

an insecticide at planting time should prevent this.

Potatoes are particularly useful for breaking new ground because their canopy shades-out weeds and the earthing-up exposes a large surface area to weathering, thus improving the soil's structure. Some gardeners maintain that soil becomes more fertile if it is mixed with a potato leaf compost, but this has not been proved.

Varieties First earlies – 'Pentland Javelin': not the earliest new potato but a heavy cropper and a good smooth, moist texture for those who do not like dry potatoes. 'Epicure': somewhat hardier. Second earlies – 'Wilja': a solid, good cooker of reasonable flavour and high yield. 'Maris Peer': has useful scab resistance, but objects to dry conditions and thin soils. Maincrop – 'Desirée': a personal favourite with superb flavour; a heavy cropper and resistant to most diseases other than scab. 'King Edward': still a favourite for its reliability and cooking quality, but it is not a heavy cropper.

RADISH

A quick growing annual root crop belonging to the cabbage family, ideal for salads. In addition to the popular round, red-skinned radishes there are several other summer types: cylindrical (or intermediate) – about the size of a thumb, red- and yellow-skinned; long – white skinned. Although they are not so often grown, there are also large winter varieties of radish, some of which have an unusual black skin.

Site and soil Rich and fertile, manured for a previous crop. Add a little fertilizer before sowing and rake the soil finely. The summer crop needs shade.

Sowing Summer varieties: in rows 15 cm (6 in) apart in drills 13 mm ($\frac{1}{2}$ in) deep. Under cloches: in January and February. Outdoors: in March. Water the drills before sowing. Sow successively at two-week intervals until the end of May – results for summer-sown seed are gener-

ally unsatisfactory – further sowings can be made from mid August to mid September. It is vital to thin the seedlings to 2·5 cm (1 in) apart. Winter varieties: rows 23 cm (9 in) apart. Sow July to early August and thin to 15 cm (6 in) apart.

For the winter varieties allow 12 plants per sq m (sq yd).

Cultivation Always keep the crop adequately watered to prevent bolting and the formation of woody roots. Keep down weeds.

Possible problems Slugs can be a nuisance, particularly with the winter types. Birds may pull out seedlings, so protect with cotton or a net. Holes in the leaves are likely to be caused by larvae of the flea beetle – spray with liquid derris or, better still, use an insecticide when sowing.

Growing time Summer varieties, 20–40 days; winter varieties: 70–84 days.

Harvesting The round, cylindrical and long types must be pulled while they are still young, before they become woody and hot flavoured. The large winter types are hardy and best left in the soil, protected by a covering of straw or peat until needed; they can be lifted and stored like carrots.

Special points Because radishes are so quick growing they are best treated as catch crops or for intercropping when other vegetables will provide some shade.

Varieties 'Cherry Belle' (round): red

Left: 'French Breakfast', a favourite radish with a crisp texture and mild flavour, provided it is not left in the ground for too long.

Right: Spinach can be sown in succession from March to May to give a steady supply through the summer.

Only pick the younger outer leaves of ruby chard. Carefully pull them off at the base of the plant to include the gorgeous red stems which can be eaten with the leaves.

skin, mild flavoured and crisp. 'French Breakfast' (cylindrical): quick growing with crimson skin and good white flesh. 'Long White Icicle' (long): white outside and nutty in flavour. 'China Rose' (winter): long, oval root, bright rose skin, crisp white flesh. 'Black Spanish Round' (winter): black skin, good flavour.

SPINACH, SPINACH BEET AND LEAF BEET

Although all the plants used as spinach are members of the fat hen family, they are not all spinach. To the true summer and winter spinach is added the New Zealand spinach, spinach beet, the 'perpetual' spinach, and leaf beet or Swiss chard which is a spinach substitute. Spinach is not to everyone's taste.

Soil Good, deeply dug soil with plenty of organic manure is essential. This is not always appreciated and is possibly why spinach often proves so difficult, easily running to seed. Leaf beet is far less demanding, easier to grow and therefore a better choice for the beginner. All spinach likes slightly acid to neutral soil and liming may therefore be necessary.

Sowing and planting Ordinary spinach: rows, 30 cm (12 in) apart; sow seed thinly, 2·5 cm (1 in) deep; thin to 15 cm (6 in). Summer spinach: sow successionally every three weeks from March to May. Winter spinach: sow August and September. New Zealand spinach: grow in stations 60 cm (2 ft) apart. Sow three seeds per station, about 20 mm ($\frac{3}{4}$ in) deep, pull out the two weakest as they grow. Sow seed in May. Leaf beet: rows, 38 cm (15 in) apart; sow seeds 10 cm (4 in) apart, 2·5 cm (1 in) deep; thin to 30 cm (12 in) apart; sow seed in April.

Allow 30 plants per sq m (sq yd) for ordinary and New Zealand spinach and three plants to the same area for leaf beet.

Cultivation Spinaches are not excessively demanding of water, but mulching will be appreciated and extra watering in dry weather to prevent bolting.

Possible problems Downy mildew makes the foliage inedible in cold wet weather. Copper spray is the only answer.

Shading will reduce bolting, so growing on the shady side of, or between, larger crops will provide this condition. Pick off any flowers to keep leaves growing. Protect winter spinach and leaf beet with cloches or by lagging the plants with straw or bracken.

Growing time Summer and winter spinach, 75 days; New Zealand spinach, 40 days; leaf beet, 100 days.

Harvesting Ordinary summer spinach from successional sowings will crop from May to November and winter spinach from November to May. In theory, this covers the whole year but, in practice, there is likely to be a short gap in May. New Zealand spinach should crop from June to about September, depending on the season. Both types should be picked carefully, nipping off the leaves without tearing. They are quite robust plants and up to half the leaves may be picked at a time.

Leaf beet can be pulled a little in the winter, but mainly in August and September. Take only the young outer leaves while they are tender and pull them off complete with the base, like rhubarb, being extra careful not to pull up the plant. Keep the pickings as clean as possible.

Special points Hungry spinach of any kind will be bitter and possibly earthy flavoured. Give extra base dressing and liquid feed well throughout the summer.

Varieties Ordinary summer spinach – 'Norvak': a new hybrid, producing large yields and slow to run to seed. Ordinary winter spinach – 'Broadleaf Prickly': a very dark green leaf, slow to run to seed (the seeds prickly, not the plant). New Zealand spinach is sold purely as that; there are no variety names. Leaf beet 'spinach' or Swiss chard, and the red-stemmed ruby chard are grown for their thick leaf stalks as well as their leaves. Spinach beet is the perpetual spinach and is grown like the chards.

SWEDE

A member of the cabbage family and closely related to the turnip, the swede is generally much hardier and milder flavoured. Like the turnip, it is not a great favourite although it was a staple food for most people up until this century. Its reputation undeservedly now rests on the unattractive way it is sometimes served up as mash, particularly by institutions. However, it is worth growing to add variety to the range of crops harvested in the winter months.

Soil Like all brassicas, swedes need firm planting in non-acid, free-draining soil which has been amply manured for the previous crop.

Sowing Rows 38 cm (15 in) apart. Sow seed thinly 13 mm ($\frac{1}{2}$ in) deep; thin seedlings gradually to leave best and strongest 23 cm (9 in) apart. Sow successively from April to June.

Allow 10 plants per sq m (sq yd).

Test for the ripeness of sweetcorn by peeling back the outer leaves and squeezing the seed. It is ready if a milky fluid is released.

Always use a fork to lift swede. Being hardy, it can be left in the soil till needed. Alternatively store in boxes of moist peat.

Cultivation Keep soil where the crop is growing evenly moist, to prevent the swedes becoming woody.

Possible problems Cabbage root fly can be a pest and is difficult to control culturally with collars. Soil insecticide, such as diazinon, may be the only answer. As with turnips, swedes are susceptible to boron deficiency, but this is more likely to affect swedes in the form of brown heart. Dissolve 36 g of borax in 10 litres (1 oz in 1 gallon) of water and apply evenly over 17 sq m (20 sq yd).

Growing time 160 days.

Harvesting Lift as required for eating from early autumn. They are completely hardy and can be left in the soil, although they will store equally well in boxes of moist peat if this is more convenient; stored dry, they tend to lose water and become tough. There is no point in freezing swedes.

Always lift with a fork, and do not pull them up.

Special points Like brassicas, swedes are very susceptible to club root. Do not grow them on the same soil each year, and dress the seed drill with lime, mercurous chloride or benomyl.

Varieties 'Marian': club root resistant and has a good flavour. 'Acme': a quick growing variety.

SWEET CORN

Sweet corn is a member of the grass family, familiar in the supermarkets but still not widely grown in home gardens. The difference in flavour of the freshly picked and cooked cobs is sufficient reason for growing it.

Soil A well drained, humus-rich, water-retentive soil is necessary for success.

Sowing and planting Sow two seeds to a peat pot of compost in a greenhouse in April for planting out in early June. Pull out the weaker seedling as soon as possible. In the garden, sow seed in May under cloches or early June in open ground. Sow in blocks rather than rows,

'Outdoor Girl', recognized by its slightly ribbed fruits, is one of the earlier outdoor tomatoes to ripen. It is a heavy cropper and has a good flavour.

perhaps among decorative garden plants, or as a windbreak, again putting two seeds in each position and removing the weaker seedling.

Transplants and seedlings should be planted 45 cm (18 in) apart in both directions to form the planting block which aids wind pollination and thus ensures a good crop.

Allow four plants per sq m (sq yd).

Cultivation Sweet corn plants root from their stems and earthing-up helps steady them in windy weather. Keep the plants well watered in dry weather and liquid feed when the cobs are forming.

Tap the plants on a dry, still day to release pollen from the male flowers at the tops. Pollen will drift down on to the 'silks' (the female flowers) below to help ensure a good set of seed.

Possible problems The maggots of fruit fly can cause, among other things, poor sized cobs; it is best to play safe by dressing the seed with an insecticide. If any swellings appear on the plants, which

is possible in hot summers, cut them off immediately and burn them. After harvesting burn the plants and do not grow sweet corn on the same plot for at least four years.

Growing time 100 days.

Harvesting When the cobs are swollen and firm peel back the outer leaves to test for ripeness. The seeds should release a milky cream when squeezed if they are ready to eat; a watery fluid means that the cob is still unripe. Another sign that the cobs are nearly ready for picking is that the fine white threads at the top of the cobs start to turn black. Pick just before needed to ensure freshness.

Special points This crop is unlikely to be successful unless grown in an open, sunny site.

Varieties 'First of All': a reliable early variety and a good choice for cooler areas. 'Northstar': for northern areas. 'Kelvedon Glory': for size and flavour.

All cordon varieties of tomato must be supported with bamboo canes and trained (see opposite page).

TRAINING CORDON TOMATOES

1. Drive in a bamboo cane, before planting seedlings. They are ready when flowers on the first truss are opening.

2. As the tomato plant grows, loosely tie the main stem to the bamboo cane, using string.

3. Where a leaf stalk joins the main stem, side shoots will grow. Pinch these out, before they grow too large, sapping strength from the plant.

TOMATO

Certain tomato varieties can be grown outdoors in mild parts of the country, given a sunny sheltered spot.

Soil During previous winter, dig garden compost and well rotted manure into the soil. Rake in a general fertilizer before planting. They can also be grown in pots or growing bags.

Sowing and planting Sow under glass at beginning of April. Set seed 2·5 cm (1 in) apart in trays of seed compost and germinate in propagator or plastic bag. Prick out into pots of potting compost. Plant out six to eight weeks after sowing, when flowers are visible on first truss. Bought, ready-grown seedlings can be planted out in late May to June. Rows 75 cm (30 in) apart for cordon varieties and 60 cm (2 ft) apart for bush varieties. Planting distance 45 cm (18 in) apart. Allow six cordon varieties per sq m (yd) and four bush varieties per sq m (yd).

Cultivation Stake cordon varieties. Remove side shoots at leaf joint and pinch out growing tips when four to six trusses have formed. Bush varieties do not need staking or pinching out. Water frequently. Feed weekly with a liquid tomato fertilizer when small tomatoes form on first truss.

Tomato seedlings can be planted in growing bags when 15–20 cm (6–8 in) tall.

'Yellow Perfection' ripens earlier and has a sweeter taste than other yellow varieties.

Bush tomatoes rarely require staking. They will grow in any sunny spot.

Possible problems Look out for aphids, grey mould, tomato leaf mould, foot rot and virus diseases.

Growing time 140 days.

Harvesting Pick in August and September when the fruit is ripe and fully coloured. Hold the fruit in hand and press the stalk with thumb to break it at the 'knuckle'. Before frost arrives, remove unripened tomatoes and ripen in a drawer alongside a ripe apple or tomato.

Varieties Cordon – 'Ailsa Craig': gives a heavy early crop of good flavoured medium-sized tomatoes. 'Alicante': resistant to greenback, is an early heavy cropping variety with excellent flavoured fruits. 'Marmande': produces large well flavoured beefsteak tomatoes. 'Sweet 100':

has cherry-sized well flavoured fruit. 'Yellow Perfection': has sweetly flavoured yellow tomatoes. Bush varieties – 'Pixie': a heavy cropper with small well flavoured fruit, ripens quickly. 'Red Alert': early maturing good cropper, small well-flavoured tomatoes. 'The Amateur': early, large crop of medium-sized tomatoes.

TURNIP

Another member of the brassica family, turnips are grown both for their roots and their tops which are used as spring greens.

Soil Like swedes and the other brassicas, turnips require a firm soil with a good residue of humus from the previous crop and sufficient lime to keep the soil neutral (pH 7 or just below).

Sowing Sow seed thinly about 13 mm ($\frac{1}{2}$ in) deep. Earlies: rows 23 cm (9 in) apart and thin the seedlings to 13 cm (5 in) apart. Under cloches in February; outdoors in March and April. Maincrop: rows 30 cm (12 in) apart and thin the seedlings to 23 cm (9 in) apart. Sow first batch March or April, then every three weeks or so until July. Spring greens: rows 7·5 cm (3 in) apart in July and August. No thinning is required. Allow 15 plants per sq m (sq yd) for roots; 40 plants for turnip tops.

Cultivation As with swedes, too little water causes woody, tough roots. Fluctuation in the soil's water supply can cause roots to split. Extra feeding with liquid seaweed or soluble fertilizer will keep the crop growing strongly.

Possible problems Soft rot causes slimy brown rot inside the turnip; outside it appears normal, but leaves droop. Damage by hoeing, too much manure and prolonged wet soil all contribute to this.

Growing time 42–82 days.

Harvesting Begin to lift early turnips when they are about egg size – at this stage they can be pulled like radishes. Lift maincrop varieties as soon as they are big enough to use, about October. They are not as hardy as swedes but in most areas they can be left in the soil until needed. In cold, wet districts lift with a fork, twist off

Above: 'Sprinter', one of the smallest and earliest of early turnip varieties.

Left: 'Golden Ball', a yellow-fleshed maincrop turnip which keeps well.

the tops and store in boxes of peat.

For spring greens, cut the leaves from March or April onwards, depending on the weather; the plants will respond to this by producing several crops of leaves.

Special points Early varieties of turnips need more care and better soil conditions than maincrop varieties.

Varieties Early – 'Snowball': the best white-fleshed early. Maincrop – 'Golden Ball': tender, yellow-fleshed, mild flavoured. Spring greens – 'Spring Top White'.

HERBS

A vegetable garden would not be complete without a small selection of culinary herbs. Either grow them in a plot on their own, perhaps in a group of small formal beds edged with clipped box or rosemary (arranged in a geometrical design reminiscent of the Elizabethan knot gardens) or have them alongside your vegetables. The ornamental herbs – thyme, sage, borage and rosemary, for example – can be cultivated in flower and shrub borders, or in pots if space in the beds is at a premium. Herbs also grow well in windowboxes.

GROWING HERBS

SITE AND SOIL
As most popular herbs come from southern Europe or the Mediterranean region, they need a sunny site sheltered from cold winds – the south or west side of the house, a wall or thick hedge are ideal. With the exception of mint, angelica and parsley, which thrive best in moderately moist soil, all the other herbs listed here need a well-drained medium which is not rich. Too rich a soil produces sappy growth of poor flavour and keeping quality.

SOWING AND PLANTING
Though most herbs can be raised from seed, it is often simpler, and certainly less trouble, to buy the plants – available in spring. With shrubby herbs like rosemary and bay, you will probably only need one plant of each. Even with the popular perennials like chives and mint, a few specimens are sufficient.

If you decide to raise the herbs from seed (see individual entries for suitable species), sow the seed in February or March in pots of seed compost. Cover the pots with a plastic bag, sheet of glass or place them in a propagator. Keep at a temperature of 18–21°C (65–70°F) out of direct sunlight.

When the seedlings appear, take them out of the propagator, or remove the glass

If there isn't room in the vegetable garden for herbs, grow them in pots and windowboxes on a sunny part of the patio. Here they will be close at hand for the cook, and their sweet fragrance can be enjoyed by anyone sitting near by.

or plastic bag and place them in a lighter spot, perhaps on a windowsill or in the greenhouse. As soon as one or two true leaves appear (after the seed leaves), prick the seedlings out into separate pots. Grow them on, then harden off in a cold frame and plant out in May. Hardy perennial herbs can also be sown directly outdoors in a seed bed in May.

CARE
Most herbs are easy to grow, given a suitable site and soil. Keep the ground around them well weeded, and pick them regularly, so their shape remains neat and compact. The more invasive plants – mint,

for example – should also be trimmed occasionally to prevent them from choking the entire bed. Every three years, the perennial herbs should be replaced, either by taking cuttings or by using division.

PROPAGATION
Perennial and shrubby herbs can be increased by division or taking cuttings. (See individual herb entries for suitable methods.)

Division In late winter and early spring, lift established clumps out of the ground. Divide them into even-sized pieces, using your hands or a fork if the

LIFTING AND DIVIDING CHIVES

1. Lift mature or overcrowded clumps of chives out of the ground, using a garden fork.

2. Divide into smaller clumps, by prising the roots apart with your hands or a small fork.

3. Plant out the new divisions, without delay, in the desired position. Make sure that the chives are well watered.

roots are entangled, and then replant in the desired position.

Cuttings Take cuttings in summer from semi-ripened shoots. Make a diagonal cut into the stem just below the junction with a side shoot; make another cut just above the junction with the side shoot. Dip the cutting in hormone rooting powder and then root it in a pot of seed compost or a half-sand, half-peat mixture.

Both the seeds and young leaves of the caraway plant can be used in cooking.

Cover the pot with a plastic bag, sealed with a rubber band and place in a cold frame or on a windowsill.

HARVESTING AND DRYING

Herbs grown for their young stems and foliage – e.g. angelica, borage, chives, fennel and parsley – must be harvested before flowering. All are best used fresh, but the last three can be dried. A few herbs are grown for their seeds, e.g. dill and

fennel. For these, the seed crop must be yellowing and starting to turn brown. Lift or cut the plants at ground level, tie them in small bundles and hang head-downwards in a warm, dry place until the seeds fall easily when you touch them. Strip the seed and store in sealed opaque jars in a cool dry place.

Bulbous herbs such as garlic are lifted when the leaves yellow, dried in the sun or in any dry place, then cleaned and hung up for use. The remaining herbs described below, though best used fresh, can be dried for winter use. Just as the plants come into flower, gather healthy sprays and space them out in trays kept in a warm airy place. An airing cupboard or the warming drawer of a stove are suitable provided there is adequate ventilation. Turn the herbs once a day until they feel brittle to the touch. Crumble them and store in opaque jars. Ideally herbs should be kept somewhere that is both cool and dark so they retain their freshness.

A–Z OF HERBS

ANGELICA
A robust, upright biennial or short-lived perennial which, if allowed to flower, reaches 1·8 m (6 ft) or more in height. It has handsome leaves divided into several leaflets and clusters of tiny greenish flowers. Only clusters of the young leaf and flower stalks are used in the kitchen. Raise new angelica plants from seed.

BASIL
This half-hardy annual, also known as sweet basil, can grow into a bushy, upright plant 60 cm (2 ft) or more in height,

TAKING CUTTINGS OF SHRUBBY HERBS

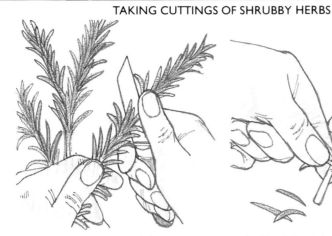

1. Take a cutting of a semi-ripened shoot in summer. Neaten off the end by making a sharp diagonal cut with a knife.

2. Carefully strip the leaves off the lower end of the cutting to leave the stem bare. Do this gently with your hands.

3. Wet the bottom end of the cutting with water and dip in a pot of hormone rooting powder to encourage roots to grow.

4. Fill trays with seed compost or a half-sand, half-peat mixture. Using a matchstick, make holes and insert the cuttings.

5. Firm in the cuttings with your fingertips, and then gently water them, using a fine rose on a watering can.

6. Cover with a clear polythene bag, keeping the polythene off the leaves. Place on a warm windowsill.

Bay, an attractive evergreen shrub or small tree, can be trained into a standard.

with small, oblong leaves in pairs. The tiny tubular flowers are white. Use the clove-scented leaves when they are young. Raise from seed.

BAY
Also know as sweet bay, this is the tree whose leaves were used to wreathe famous people in ancient Greece. Although an almost hardy evergreen tree, it stands clipping well and can be easily rooted from cuttings so it is not necessary to provide a lot of room for its growth. The aromatic leaves are best used when newly matured. Propagate by taking cuttings.

BORAGE
A decorative hardy annual up to 60 cm (2 ft) tall, but often less. It has large, rough, oval leaves smelling of cucumber and sprays of sky-blue starry flowers used for decorating desserts and summer cocktails. Raise from seed.

CARAWAY
This hardy annual forms slim stems 60 cm (2 ft) or more in height, bearing ferny leaves and topped by flat heads of tiny white flowers. Its seeds are used in cooking, but young leaves can be chopped and added to salads. Raise from seed.

CHERVIL
Similar in overall appearance to caraway, this biennial reaches about 45 cm (18 in) and is grown for its parsley-flavoured leaves. Raise from seed.

CHIVES
This densely tufted perennial has grassy, hollow leaves 25 cm (10 in) long with a delicate onion flavour. If allowed to develop, 2·5 cm (1 in) wide globular heads of small rose-purple flowers top the foliage. Ideally, pinch out the flower spikes when small to promote more leaves, and use young leaves in preference to mature ones. Raise from seed or propagate by division.

COMFREY
A tall wide-spreading perennial which has coarse, rough leaves, blue or creamy white flowers and reaches 60–90 cm (2–3 ft) high. It is used as a medicinal herb and can be cooked like spinach or added to a salad. Raise from seed.

CORIANDER
An annual grown mainly for its spicy, aromatic seeds, though the leaves are sometimes used as a garnish. Grow in full sun in a light rich soil, sowing the seeds in very early spring. Plants can be thinned to 10–15 cm (4–6 in) apart. When seeds have turned a light greyish-brown, cut down the plant and leave to dry for two or three days. When dry, shake out seeds and store. Raise from seed.

CUMIN
A slender annual reaching 30–60 cm (1–2 ft), the plant has long thin leaves and small pink or white flowers. Cumin is grown for its seed alone. Raise from seed.

DILL
Much like fennel but with a single stem reaching 90 cm (3 ft) high, this annual is grown for its aniseed-flavoured leaves and seeds. Raise from seed.

FENNEL
This is a graceful clump-forming perennial which can be grown for decoration as well as edible values. Its dark, almost blue-green, sweetly aromatic leaves are finely divided. The flowering stems are best removed when young, unless seed is required. Allowed to grow unrestricted,

The graceful, finely divided leaves of fennel make it a suitable herb to grow as a feature, surrounded by a low-clipped hedge.

Left: For a regular supply of chives, remove the flowerheads before they open and cut the leaves when they are still young.

Here, a simple but stunning herb garden has been created by growing the clumps of herbs between paving slabs. Where a large bed was needed, several slabs were lifted and the ground underneath prepared for cultivation.

VEGETABLE GARDENING

When the leaves on garlic plants turn yellow in July or August, lift the plants and hang them up to dry in the sun.

fennel will reach 1·5–2·5 m (5–8 ft) high and produce flattened heads of tiny yellowish flowers. Raise from seed or propagate by division.

GARLIC
The familiar white bulb of this plant is composed of several narrow bulblets known as cloves. The narrow leaves grow to 45 cm (18 in) tall. Sometimes, rounded heads of tiny, white, purple-tinged flowers are produced on stems above the leaves. Propagate by separating the cloves and replanting them.

HORSERADISH
A hardy perennial with large floppy leaves growing from the base of the plant to a height of 60–90 cm (2–3 ft). The flowers are white on a single stem but do not appear every season. The large thick roots are used for cooking. Plant out young shoots, or bury pieces of root.

HYSSOP
This hardy perennial grows up to 45 cm (18 in) in height. With its woody growth, technically it is a low shrub but it needs annual pruning to keep it low and compact. The narrow, aromatic leaves are in opposite pairs, and small tubular blue, pink or white flowers form showy upright spikes. Both leaves and flowers can be used to flavour stews and salads. Raise from seed or take cuttings.

LEMON BALM
Sometimes simply known as balm, this is a clump-forming hardy perennial with pairs of corrugated lemon-scented oval leaves and clusters of small, tubular, white flowers which form leafy spikes. The leaves can be used fresh or dried. Raise from seed or propagate by division.

LOVAGE
In leaf, this clump-forming perennial resembles celery. It will send up stems 2·5 m (8 ft) high which branch and bear clusters of yellowish flowers. Both the seeds and leaves are used. Raise from seed.

MARJORAM
Usually listed as sweet marjoram, this is a shrubby-based perennial grown as a half-hardy annual from seed. It has slender stems about 45 cm (18 in) tall with pairs of oval leaves and loose clusters of small, knotted flower spikes bearing minute white or pinkish flowers. Its leaves are mainly used for flavouring meat dishes. Raise from seed.

MINT
There are several different kinds of mint. All are hardy perennials 60–90 cm (2–3 ft) high and all can be invasive. They have opposite pairs of simple leaves and spikes of tiny, tubular, mauve flowers. Common spearmint is the form most usually grown, with smooth, bright green lance-shaped leaves. Apple mint has broadly oblong to rounded, white, hairy leaves. Peppermint yields the world's supply of peppermint oil. It is similar to spearmint (one of its parents) but is easily distinguished by its smell. Propagate by division.

PARSLEY
This familiar hardy biennial, which can also be grown as an annual, forms a tufted rosette of finely cut leaves which are flat in the original species but in the best known varieties are 'crested' or mossy. If allowed to flower it produces an upright branched stem to 45 cm (18 in) or more with tiny yellowish flowers. Parsley is a good plant for edging the herb garden, and is ideal for growing in a container. Raise from seed.

PURSLANE
An attractive tender annual with succulent leaves, small yellow flowers, and upright reddish stems, purslane grows up to 15 cm (6 in) high. It has a sharp clean flavour which is best combined with other herbs. It is essentially a salad herb but the young shoots can be cooked as a vegetable. Purslane must not be sown until

One sage plant will usually provide enough leaves for a household. Every summer after flowering, trim the plant to keep it neat. As it is not long-lived, replace every three years.

Grow purslane, a slightly tender evergreen, in a sunny sheltered site.

May when all danger of frost has passed. It needs sandy soil with a sunny aspect. Raise from seed.

ROSEMARY
A bushy evergreen shrub reaching up to 1·5 m (5 ft) or more high, this herb has dark, almost needle-like leaves and lavender, sage-like flowers. The leaves go well with meat dishes. Propagate by taking cuttings.

RUE
This 60 cm (2 ft) high evergreen shrub is primarily grown for its dissected blue-grey leaves and open clusters of yellow flowers with cupped petals. The pungent smelling foliage can be used to flavour egg and fish dishes. Propagate by taking cuttings.

SAGE
Like mint and parsley, this is a very popular herb. It is an evergreen shrub reaching 60 cm (2 ft) high with finely wrinkled grey-green leaves and spikes of quite large, tubular, two-lipped blue-purple flowers. Raise from seed or propagate by taking cuttings.

SALAD BURNET
A clump-forming hardy perennial, reach-

Parsley grows best in rich soil in a shaded site. Raise it from seed for picking that year.

If growing herbs in a large border, set the tallest ones – fennel, for example – at the back and the shorter clump-forming varieties towards the front, so each plant receives maximum sunlight.

ing 60 cm (2 ft) or more when in bloom. The leaves are composed of 9–21 oval leaflets and have an almost fern-like quality. The flowering stems are best removed when young to promote more young leaves, for harvesting and use in salads and sauces. Raise from seed or propagate by division.

SAVORY

There are two kinds of savory: summer and winter. Winter savory is a small hardy, wiry shrub 15–30 cm (6–12 in) tall with small narrow leaves and short spikes of small, pale purple flowers. Summer savory is a slender, upright hardy annual with similar but longer leaves and white to pale purple flowers. The leaves of both are used in fish, egg and salad dishes. Raise from seed or propagate by cuttings.

SORREL

A low growing herb with acid tasting leaves. It is commonly used in salads and in soups. Raise from seed.

SWEET CICELY

A slow growing perennial which may reach a height of 60–150 cm (2–5 ft). It is a fragrant plant with a sweet aniseed flavour and can be used in salads or omelettes. Cut off any small white flowers as they appear; this will help the leaves retain a stronger flavour. Raise from seed.

TARRAGON

This not quite fully hardy perennial forms wide clumps of upright stems about 60 cm (2 ft) high. The narrow lance-shaped leaves are a greyish-green and an essential constituent of *fines herbes*. Small, green-ish, bobble-like flower-heads may appear in good seasons. Propagate by taking cuttings of rooted shoots.

THYME

Several sorts of thyme have herbal uses, but the two most popular are common thyme and lemon thyme. Common thyme produces hardy, wiry, spreading ever-green shrublets to 20 cm (8 in) or more in height with tiny leaves and small pale purple to whitish flowers. Its leaves are grey-green, finely hairy and aromatic.

Lemon thyme has a low-growing neat habit and bears clusters of deep pink flowers. A mild-flavoured herb, it can be used in savoury dishes or in sweet jellies, desserts and drinks. Propagate both common and lemon thyme by division or taking cuttings.

PESTS AND DISEASES

In extreme cases pests and diseases can cause havoc in the vegetable patch. But if you take simple measures to prevent their arrival in the first place, can recognize the pests and diseases if they do occur, and are well prepared to deal with them, they shouldn't be a problem.

GENERAL PREVENTION

By following a few basic rules, it is possible to greatly reduce the likelihood of pests and diseases in your plot.

HEALTHY SOIL

A healthy, well-fed soil with sufficient manure and fertilizer will grow strong disease- and pest-resistant plants. It is worth remembering, however, that lush and over-fed specimens will also be susceptible to attack, so check your plants regularly – at least once a week.

HYGIENE

Keep your garden clean. Rotting cabbage and rhubarb leaves will harbour diseases and pests. Weeds, likewise, are often 'host plants' carrying pests and diseases to infest your crop. Even dry debris, such as stones, bricks and wood, provides hiding places for slugs, earwigs, millepedes and woodlice, all of which attack plants.

CROP ROTATION

This method of cultivation helps to prevent a build-up of a particular pest or disease, though in today's smaller gardens it may not be as effective as it was in the larger plots of the past.

CAREFUL HANDLING

Damaged plants attract pests and encourage disease. Avoid bruising, cutting or crushing them. Thin, pick and hoe between crops with care.

SOWING THINLY

Sown too thickly, seed rots easily below ground and seedlings are prone to the damping-off disease. Sowing more thickly than recommended is a good way of getting an additional early crop from the same ground, so you need to strike a balance.

CHOOSING CROPS AND VARIETIES

Some crops are more resilient and many varieties are specially bred for pest and disease resistance of one kind or another. The potato 'Pentland Javelin', for instance, is resistant to scab, and some tomato varieties have virus, eelworm, wilt and 'greenback' resistance. Make sure the variety is suitable for growing in your area. Some varieties only flourish in a particular type of soil or climate, so check carefully before you buy any seeds or

Scarecrows will only deter birds effectively if they are moved occasionally.

seedlings. Always read any accompanying labels or instructions.

PROTECTION
Building a high windbreak around the vegetable garden will prevent a great many pests blowing in, but in many cases this is difficult. It's far easier simply to erect a polythene screen around vegetables likely to be affected: carrots and celery, for example, can be hidden from their respective flies which search at or just above ground level looking for food. This, in turn, prevents the flies from laying eggs on the topsoil, so that the roots are then less likely to be eaten by grubs.

Cabbage flies will not be deterred by a polythene screen but you can at least prevent them from laying their eggs in the soil near the base of the brassica stems. Place some carpet underlay, cut in circles with a central hole and a radial split joining this to the circumference, around the young cabbage stems, or buy cabbage collars which serve a similar purpose.

DISGUISE
By planting certain crops together (see Intersowing page 24) one crop can be used to disguise the smell of the other from a potential pest. Spring onions, for example, will disguise the smell of carrots and deter carrot fly. This is not considered a very

Leatherjackets tunnel into root crops and eat the stems and lower leaves.

88

ABOVE-GROUND PESTS

Greenfly Small greenfly aphids usually appear outside in the spring, or throughout the year in greenhouses. Spray outside plants with an insecticide such as menazon or diazinon.

Black bean aphids These sap plants of energy. Outside plants are vulnerable between May and July. Before flowering, treat them with an insecticide like pirimphosmethyl.

Cabbage whitefly Found on undersides of the leaves of cabbages, Brussels sprouts and other brassicas, and appear from May to September. Spray with dimetheote.

Caterpillars Appearing from March onwards, they eat holes in the leaves of most plant varieties. Remove by hand or treat with derris or malathion.

Celery fly Maggots appear in April and leave brown blotches on celery and parsnip leaves. They may kill the plant. Treat crops with malathion.

Earwigs Eat beetroot, carrot and parsnip leaves, making ragged holes. They appear between May and October. Dust or spray with malathion or HCH.

Flea beetles Cabbages, turnips and radishes can be affected in May. They make small holes in young leaves. Dust seedlings with derris to prevent damage.

Pea thrips Live on pea foliage, and leave a silvery trace behind. They like hot, dry summer weather. Dust or spray plants with malathion or HCH.

Pea and bean weevils Eat the edges of pea and bean leaves in a semi-circular pattern, between March and June. Dust young plants with HCH immediately.

A colony of aphids on Brussels sprout leaves. Spray them immediately as they will weaken the plant and may be carrying viral diseases.

reliable method of control. Only one out of ten trials seems to work. A better way of dispersing the plant smells which attract pests is, after thinning seedlings, to water the row thoroughly and firm in the seedlings well.

DETERRING BIRDS
The most practical bird scarers are the quiet ones like scarecrows, flapping polythene strips or tin foil discs and, more recently, imitation birds of prey. Research has shown that even these are only effective if they are moved about from time to time; otherwise the birds soon become accustomed to them.

A variation on the scarecrow theme is a

BELOW-GROUND PESTS

Cutworm Eat through lettuce shoots at ground level in early spring and late summer. Weed to reduce the risk of infestation. Alternatively, work bromophos well into the soil.

Cabbage root fly Newly transplanted brassicas such as Brussels sprouts will collapse if attacked by the maggots of this fly. Protect between April and September by applying diazinon.

Carrot fly Celery, carrots and parsnips are damaged by tunnelling carrot fly maggots. Water plants with diazinon two or three times in August and September to prevent damage.

Chafer grubs Curved in shape and over an inch long, they feed on a variety of roots. Use a soil fumigant on the larvae and kill beetles by spraying stems with BHC.

Leatherjackets The larvae of craneflies, these appear between April and June, usually in wet weather. They attack most vegetables. Protect with diazinon.

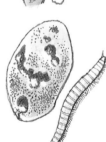

Millepedes Tunnel into potatoes and other root crops during late summer and autumn. Deep cultivation in well-manured soil should help to keep them at bay.

Onion fly Between May and August their small, white maggots feed on decaying onion, leek or shallot tissues. Water roots two or three times with trichlorphon.

Potato cyst eelworm Potatoes and tomatoes are susceptible to these pests between July and September. In severe cases, do not plant on the site for five years.

Root aphids White colonies affect the young shoots of broad beans from May to July outdoors, causing leaves to yellow and wilt. Water roots with diazinon.

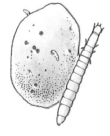

Wireworms These feed mostly on tubers, stems and roots of potatoes, tomatoes and lettuces. HCH can be applied to susceptible crops.

Slugs and snails Leave a trail of slime and damage the leaves, stems and roots of a variety of vegetables. Water soil with a liquid slug (and snail) killer.

Woodlice Generally attack seedlings and young plants in greenhouses at night. Dust or water soil around seed boxes with BHC to deter them.

special wire which, when tightly stretched across the plot, produces a humming sound in the wind that keeps birds away. Black cotton, zig-zagged across the plot – another alternative – is frowned on by conservationists because birds can easily become entangled in it – a particular problem if the thread used is an indestructible synthetic material, which can kill the birds. But a single strand of real black cotton 2·5–5 cm (1–2 in) above a row of seeds or seedlings is most effective, as the birds dislike having to avoid it while they attempt to feed.

If pigeons are a problem the only effective answer is to thoroughly net over the plants. It's worth doing, though, as a couple of pigeons are capable of completely devastating a brassica bed, stripping every leaf to a bare rib.

DETERRING MAMMAL PESTS
The damage caused by dogs and cats is often difficult to repair. They also represent a health and hygiene hazard so some form of prevention is essential. Pepper sometimes deters them, but it is not always effective. Renardine works reasonably consistently on all larger mammals (rabbits, mice and moles included), but it does have an unpleasant smell when used in large quantities. Small stakes with a renardine-soaked sacking strip wrapped around their tops, pushed into the soil at

Look out for cabbage white caterpillars on brassica leaves between April and October. The first indication of their presence will be holes in the leaves.

intervals around the plot, will keep the mammals away most effectively. Alternatively, you can soak a single strand of thick hairy string in the liquid and lay this along the soil of a seed row or seedling bed to deter mice. (Make sure you keep the string off the plants.)

To deter moles mix a tablespoon of renardine into a jam jar full of sharp sand. Tightly seal the jar, and keep it handy so that at the first sign of a mole hill you can

put a spoonful of the mixture down the hole beneath the hill. Make sure that the tunnel is completely open and not blocked by earth, so the smell can spread throughout the mole run. You're unlikely to have trouble from moles after that.

CURATIVE MEASURES

If, in spite of preventive measures, pests still arrive, there are two ways of getting rid of them: cultural and insecticidal.

CULTURAL CONTROL
These are methods which encourage nature to prevent the pest problems.

Birds A vast number of caterpillars and aphids are consumed by birds so it pays to encourage them to feed in your vegetable patch. The problem for the gardener is attracting the beneficial birds without exposing your crop to the ravages of pigeons. Nesting boxes with the right-sized holes and careful feeding of favoured species (leaving out fat for blue tits, for example) can work, but the unwanted bird species are bound to appear from time to time so other cultural practices will also be necessary.

Exposing pests Digging and hoeing to expose underground pests will make a bird's job easier. You'll find that just as the

Slug damage on radishes. To prevent slugs arriving in the first place, keep garden rubbish well away from the vegetable patch. If you see any slime trails, lay slug pellets around the plants.

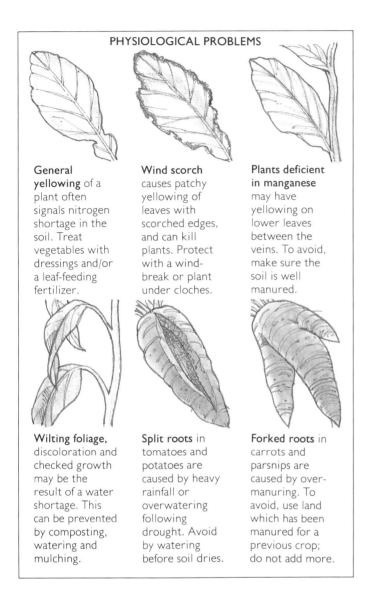

PHYSIOLOGICAL PROBLEMS

General yellowing of a plant often signals nitrogen shortage in the soil. Treat vegetables with dressings and/or a leaf-feeding fertilizer.

Wind scorch causes patchy yellowing of leaves with scorched edges, and can kill plants. Protect with a wind-break or plant under cloches.

Plants deficient in manganese may have yellowing on lower leaves between the veins. To avoid, make sure the soil is well manured.

Wilting foliage, discoloration and checked growth may be the result of a water shortage. This can be prevented by composting, watering and mulching.

Split roots in tomatoes and potatoes are caused by heavy rainfall or overwatering following drought. Avoid by watering before soil dries.

Forked roots in carrots and parsnips are caused by over-manuring. To avoid, use land which has been manured for a previous crop; do not add more.

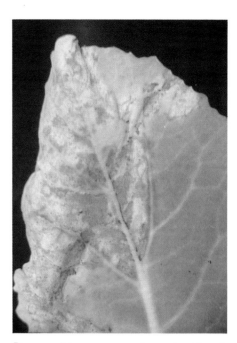

Downy mildew occurs on the undersides of leaves – it often produces a downy outgrowth.

thetic chemical insecticides, plant extracts, and natural organic soaps.

Synthetic chemical insecticides A simple selection of four will give good all-round pest control: a soil insecticide, such as bromophos or diazinon; a slug bait, based on methiocarb; a specific aphid (greenfly) spray like pirimicarb, which does not affect any other insects; and a general insecticide for caterpillars and other pests, either containing the systemic insecticide dimethoate, or the contact insecticides permethrin or resmethrin. Systemic insecticides are taken into the plant's sap and kill insects which later suck it. Contact insecticides kill only those pests that are sprayed with it.

Plant-extract insecticides are used by gardeners who regard synthetic chemical insecticides as harmful under any circumstances. The common plant extracts are rotenone, sold as derris dust and liquid derris; and pyrethrum, which is sometimes sold under that name, in dust and spray form. The third plant extract insecticide is quassia, but this is not so widely available. All three are most effective as caterpillar, greenfly and fly killers. They are contact insecticides, killing only those pests which are actually sprayed.

seagulls follow the plough, so will the robin sit close by and pick up cutworms and grubs, as well as fly pupae. After the day's digging, shrews will come out in the evening and lend a hand.

Hand picking A daily walk around the plot is useful for spotting pests before they become a problem. Look out for caterpillars and slugs on plants, and pick them off. If you come across a small colony of blackfly on a broad bean shoot, or a clutch of small orange cabbage white butterfly eggs on the underside of a leaf, rub them off between your thumb and forefinger.

In the soil, pick out caterpillars, grubs and slugs while digging and cultivating. With a sharp eye you may also spot slug or snail eggs: little clusters of white pearls.

A minor variation on hand picking is

shoot picking: blackfly are often found on the tips of broad bean shoots, for instance. If you pick off the shoots with the blackfly you eradicate the blackfly and remove the succulent shoot which attracted them in the first place.

Stale seed bed This technique of weed control, which allows weeds to germinate before burning them to the ground (see page 33) is also a good way of controlling pests as it discourages many pests which would otherwise feed on the weed roots until the vegetables arrive.

INSECTICIDAL CONTROLS
Modern insecticides are safe used carefully and wisely, when a pest is multiplying too rapidly to control by other means. Nowadays, there is a choice between syn-

PLANT DISEASES

Anthracnose Patchy brown sunken areas may appear at any time on dwarf and runner beans. Destroy diseased plants and sow in a new site. Apply carbendazim, if necessary.

Blotchy ripening Sometimes parts of developing fruit fail to ripen. Frequent watering and shading the fruit in hot weather will help prevent this, or try growing another variety.

Chocolate spot In spring, beans may become covered with chocolate brown blotches – signalling potash deficiency. Prevent it by sowing early under shelter.

Cucumber mosaic virus This virus also affects raspberries and causes yellow mottling on fruit and leaves. Control insects which carry the disease by spraying.

Foot rot This discoloration and rotting at the base of the stem can kill tomato, pea and bean plants. Treat plants by watering with cheshunt compound.

Parsnip canker These orange-brown or black cankers rot parsnip roots. Prevent by them by dressing the soil with lime and sulphate of potash.

Black leg Affects potatoes in June, developing at the base of the stem. The leaves yellow and the stem dies. Plants should be destroyed and healthy tubers replanted.

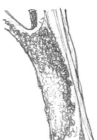

Botrytis This grey mould affects tomatoes and, in wet weather, pea and bean pods. Prevent by having good ventilation and avoid overcrowding. Burn any diseased vegetables.

Club root Roots swell and decay, and leaves yellow. Lift and burn diseased plants. Dress soil with lime and/or put four per cent calomel dust in the new planting holes.

Damping-off Young lettuces are particularly susceptible: stems decay and seedlings collapse. To avoid, sterilize compost and do not overcrowd or overwater.

Halo blight French and runner beans are susceptible to these dark, circled spots. Blistered seeds should not be planted. Spray diseased plants with copper fungicide.

Potato blight Black spotting of leaves, withering of the stem and rotting of tubers or fruit are signs from May to August. Spray stems with copper compound.

Blossom end rot This is a circular brown patch at the blossom end of developing tomatoes and can be prevented by regular watering. If the soil is acid, add garden lime.

Brown heart This internal root decay affects turnips, swedes and beetroots. Regular watering prevents it; or sprinkle topsoil with powdered borax before sowing.

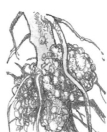

Crown gall These large, harmless galls sometimes develop on roots of fruit and vegetables in the growing season. Cut off and burn, provided doing so will not damage the fruit.

Downy mildew This furry coating appears on onions and the underside of brassica, lettuce and spinach leaves. Treat spinach and onions with zineb, and lettuces with thiram.

Leaf spot This is revealed by dark, irregular spotting. Diseased leaves should be removed and burnt, and the affected plants sprayed with a fungicide.

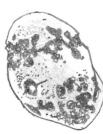

Potato scab These rust-coloured fungal scabs appear on potatoes – which can still be used, if peeled. Grow potatoes in slightly acid soil. Peat helps prevent infection.

PLANT DISEASES

Sclerotinia disease In spring and summer, tomato plants may develop stem rot. White fluffy fungus appears on the rotting stem. Affected matter should be destroyed.

Whiptail This deficiency is likely to develop in cauliflowers and broccoli. Leaves become thin and curl. Water infected vegetables with sodium molybate.

Tomato blight Outdoor tomatoes with blight gradually turn brown and rot. Spray with copper compound once a fortnight in damp weather.

White rot This white fungus rots onions, leeks, shallots and garlic, and contaminates the bed for eight years. Burn the crop and dust new seed drills with benomyl.

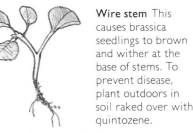

Violet root rot Asparagus is prone to develop this. Purple threads cover the roots and kill the plant. Infected plants must be destroyed and the bed not re-used.

Wire stem This causes brassica seedlings to brown and wither at the base of stems. To prevent disease, plant outdoors in soil raked over with quintozene.

Natural organic soaps are an old method of controlling pests, now seeing a return in popularity. Their insecticidal properties have been known since pre-Victorian days. The soaps available now are contact insecticides only. They will not affect insects beneficial to your vegetables to any degree because such insects are generally larger, have a more resistant body structure and are faster moving.

Fatty acids attack the cell structure of the pest rather than its nervous system or body chemistry so, unlike chemical pesticides, the pests cannot become immune to them. When applied, the soaps also decay rapidly to form simple carbon dioxide.

PLANT DISEASES

FUNGUS DISEASES

Fungi are responsible for many of the plant diseases which occur in the vegetable plot: mildew, chocolate spot and grey mould for example. The part of the fungus which you usually see on your crop is only the fruit, not the entire fungus plant. The growing part (equivalent of a normal plant's stem and leaves) is inside the leaf or whichever part of your plant is affected. Unlike pests, therefore, which can only be sprayed after the insects are seen, it is imperative that fungus diseases are prevented from becoming established by cultural means and by preventative spraying.

The weather, temperature, soil condition, planting distance, season and variety of crop all determine the likelihood of fungus diseases occurring. Powdery mildew for example thrives on warm days and cool nights and is not dependent on damp conditions. Downy mildew, the bane of lettuce, however, is a warm, moist-weather disease, as is potato blight, which can also attack tomatoes. Knowing the conditions that encourage fungus diseases will help you identify them if they arrive and point you towards the best treatment.

Choosing resistant vegetable varieties; planting or thinning sufficiently to obtain good air circulation through the crop; ventilating young plants when they are in the greenhouse; keeping soils and composts evenly watered; protecting from cold with cloches or covers, using the greenhouse, and taking care in handling and cultivating seedlings and plants all help to keep potential fungus diseases at bay. Sooner or later, however, a fungicide spray will probably be needed.

Fungicides Four fungicides should take care of all the common fungus diseases: fungicides which contain benomyl, thiophanate-methyl, bupirimate and triforine as their active ingredients are still reasonable mildew preventers despite their age. Mancozeb is also a reasonable rust control.

Copper oxychloride is used for preventing damping-off disease developing in seeds and seedlings.

Sulphur is a more natural fungicide and, since the death of the smelly lime sulphur, which was also a little dangerous to plants, it is only available as the unmodified element. Today there are micronized or colloidal sulphurs which, mixed with natural soaps and sticking agents, give much better leaf cover and persistence as well as penetrating the leaf pores to give some curative effect as well as protection.

VIRUS DISEASES

Once a plant has a virus disease there is nothing the gardener or even the professional grower can do about it. For the amateur gardener the only two courses of action are prevention and destruction.

Viruses are spread mainly by aphids and some by eelworms. Spraying and cultural controls (see page 90) will prevent serious aphid infestations. Rotation and avoiding susceptible crops are the only precautions against eelworms.

Burn infected plants if possible or at least put them in the dustbin for removal.

BACTERIAL DISEASES

While fungi and viruses are by far the most important causes of diseases in vegetables, bacteria (notably cucumber canker) can sometimes be a problem. In common with other bacterial diseases there is no satisfactory cure. It is best prevented by using sterile compost and watering accurately, especially around the plant's stem collar, where it touches the soil.

INDEX

ACKNOWLEDGEMENTS

The Publishers wish to thank the following photographers and organizations for their kind permission to reproduce the following pictures in this book:
Eric Crichton 15, 21, 22, 23t, 25, 27, 28, 38, 38, 39, 44, 47b, 49l, 50, 53, 56, 58, 67b, 70c, 76, 78t, 84; Photos Horticultural 6, 9, 14b, 33, 36b, 41, 46, 48, 52b, 57, 65b, 68b, 71tr, 72r, 88, 90b, 91; The Harry Smith Collection 32, 34, 59, 64t, 66b, 71r, 74b, 75, 77r, 81, 82b, 85tl & b, 87, 89, 90t; Suttons Seeds Ltd 61b, 65t, 78b; Sue Stickland 13.

The following photographs were specially taken for the Octopus Publishing Group Picture Library: Michael Boys 18, 19, 24, 29, 40, 43, 47t, 49r, 61t, 63b, 66t, 70t, 74t, 79, 80, 82t, 83, 86; Jerry Harpur 17, 20, 36t, 42, 63t; Neil Holmes 31, 37, 45, 51, 52t, 62, 68t, 69, 70b, 72l, 85tr; John Rigby 8; George Wright 10, 14t & c, 23b, 30, 60, 64b, 67t, 71l, 73, 77l.